T0128281

I MET GOD
AND ALSO
SATAN

*The Out-of-Body
Experience
That Dramatically
Changed My Life*

GLENN WALLING

WESTBOW
PRESS®
A DIVISION OF THOMAS NELSON
& ZONDERVAN

WestBow Press books may be ordered through booksellers or by contacting:

WestBow Press
A Division of Thomas Nelson & Zondervan
1663 Liberty Drive
Bloomington, IN 47403
www.westbowpress.com
844-714-3454

Scripture taken from the New King James Version®. Copyright © 1982
by Thomas Nelson. Used by permission. All rights reserved.

ISBN: 978-1-6642-0745-5 (sc)
ISBN: 978-1-6642-0746-2 (hc)
ISBN: 978-1-6642-0744-8 (e)

Library of Congress Control Number: 2020918907

Print information available on the last page.

WestBow Press rev. date: 10/19/2020

CONTENTS

Introduction vii

Chapter 1   Another Dimension 1
Chapter 2   The Boundaries of Reality 7
Chapter 3   The Descartes Experiment 15
Chapter 4   Not Alone 23
Chapter 5   Sent Back 27
Chapter 6   Supernatural Logic 33
Chapter 7   The Big Bang Theory 41
Chapter 8   Science Demands a Creator 47
Chapter 9   The Greatest Eclipse 59
Chapter 10   Ticket to Permanent Paradise 65
Chapter 11   Good and Bad Things, Good and Bad People 83
Chapter 12   Return Visit 97

Conclusion 99

INTRODUCTION

The out-of-this-world experience at the heart of the following pages is described in detail, precisely the way it happened. There are no embellishments, nor is any part of that fateful experience omitted.

What happened—that is, what I experienced and saw during that very extraordinary experience—could very easily be embellished to create an attention-riveting novel, or even a series of novels. However, that is not the purpose of this writing. Many years ago, when the experience occurred, those I shared it with, including religious people, were frightened and closed their ears to me. Therefore, as a young man I made a decision to protect my personal, worldly credibility and keep it to myself. I understand that it is possible keeping it secret was okay with God because times and societal acceptance standards weren't right back then. I also understand that without God's approval, I may have been hiding this experience under a bush, as Christians may say.

In any event, whether God has decided that the time is right, or He just ran out of patience with me, God Himself has directed this writing as my testimony regarding the actual encounter between Him and me. Because the purpose of this writing is not entertainment but my simple testimony as to the facts of that encounter, the potential for embellishment has been completely avoided.

The reality-expanding experience described within the following pages happened exactly as presented, down to the smallest detail.

I can assure you that not one slightest detail of that experience could ever be forgotten. I can still see and feel every action and sensation that occurred as part of that fateful and surprising venture outside of the boundaries of the physical universe in which I encountered the most powerful, unearthly principalities. Yes, the use of the plural is intentional. I met not only God Himself but Satan as well.

The names of the human participants in this venture and mentioned in the following pages have been changed.

The experience is presented as directed, through discussions with the atheist professor. These discussions are mere highlights and critical portions of many such exchanges of words and thoughts that have occurred since I became compelled to share this experience. It is the most powerful experience of my decades of life—the encounter with Almighty God Himself.

1

ANOTHER DIMENSION

I was in the spirit.
—Revelations 1:10 (NKJV)

"The group of objects coming into view out of the darkness that was surrounding me, began moving, and one of them, the light bulb, slowly came forward. I noticed that behind it, the compass began to come forward. Then a measuring scale separated itself out of the group and fell in line behind the light and the compass. This line of objects moved toward me like a line of objects on a conveyor belt, but there was no conveyor belt.

"I was so fascinated by the chorus line of objects gliding directly toward my face that I could not move or think of anything else. It was as though they had a life and purpose of their own. I didn't know where they were coming from or what force was behind them. As the light bulb approached my nose, it was hard to breathe. I didn't know whether it would stop, disappear, or crash into my face.

"Behind the light bulb, the line became longer and longer as single objects such as an eraser, a book, a clothes hangar, and many more fell in line. The whole line began moving faster and faster. I could not alter my concentration because my fascination was stronger than the fright. My full attention was on the light bulb accelerating toward my nose. Just as—"

"Okay, okay," interrupted the square-jawed Dr. Kyle sitting behind his large mahogany desk in front of matching and fully stocked bookshelves. "I am fascinated with the action scene you are describing, Glenn, but please remember that I am a professor of logic and mathematics. Instead of discussing some intriguing point of rational and logical enlightenment, you have been telling me this fantastic story that sounds more like some sort of fantasy completely outside the world of logic from where you started.

"I have been listening so far because you began by telling me about how the quote 'I think therefore I am' by the famous philosopher Descartes had intrigued you so much that you conducted an experiment to test it. Now, let's either resume the discussion of the logic test of Descartes's quote, or I will have to excuse you while I get back to work."

When I first noticed that an entire section of the bookshelves behind him was dedicated strictly to books written by the esteemed Dr. Kyle himself, I told myself that he must have ego issues. Then again, if I had written that many published books, I might set aside a similar area for them among my book collection. I wondered if my quick inclination to critique Dr. Kyle's ego was in reality some sort of subconscious effort to dispel the initial intimidation I had felt upon entering his office. I had obtained my appointment with him in the pursuit of two goals. First, his acknowledgment and acceptance of the uncommon venture I had taken outside the physical world. And second, an agreement by the extremely reputable professor of logic that the aforementioned venture was significant in reaching logical conclusions regarding the boundaries of reality, as well as the existence and relevance of God. When I had first entered his office, before noticing his bookshelf organization, I was struck by his piercing dark eyes set behind black-rimmed glasses, his jet-black hair, his deeply tanned skin, the dark-wood furniture, the brown carpet, and walls of various shades of brown. The only bright spots with the potential to shine at least a little hope into the atmosphere were his long-sleeve light blue shirt to brighten up the dark-gray slacks, the light background in the pictures and degree plaques on the walls, and the view from the window facing the ocean. If I wanted to achieve my goals in talking to Dr. Kyle, I would have to make an effort to maintain my confidence and remain calm and cool. At least my blue and light tan Hawaiian shirt with light tan cotton slacks and Rockport loafers would not only brighten up the mood of the room but also remind me that I dressed the way I liked to dress because, through much searching and effort over the years, I had derived at least some level of confidence myself.

It's a good thing confidence can be independent of looks. Even though I had been voted "boy with the prettiest eyes" back in sixth grade, that turned out to be more of a blow to my early confidence development rather than a boost, because it made me the object of laughter and ridicule among my peer group of eleven-year-old boys in that small country town. I sported my own dark brown hair and a somewhat rugged Celtic skin that had barely survived severe teenage acne and was now a bit leathered by the southern California sun.

"Dr. Kyle," I said, "I am disappointed. I have heard you have a reputation for examining tracks of thought and reason that may be considered unconventional by some. The story I am telling you is absolutely factual. It describes part of what happened during the logic test I was conducting regarding the truth of Descartes's quote about whether we think because we are, or whether we are because we think. Unfortunately, you are sounding just like the other faculty I took this to many years ago when I was a college student. Their reactions left me all alone to deal with the occurrence of an uncommon, otherworldly, yet very real and gripping event for years following.

"However, there is a difference today. I did obtain my bachelor's degree in mathematics and logic. Due to the results of that logical test of Descartes's quote those many years ago, which I was forced to keep to myself in order to retain basic credibility among the supposed rational thinkers of the day, I have done some independent studying of logic and known phenomena. If we can discuss to your satisfaction the rules and application of logic together and reach some agreements in that regard, will you allow me to finish the description of the results of that logic test of Descartes's quote, so we can evaluate it together?"

"Wow, Glenn. You've been able to maintain my interest after all. It is an excellent idea to come to agreement about rational and logical steps to evaluate the difference between truth and fiction. Is that what you mean?"

"Well, those were not exactly my words. They sound a little tougher than I had in mind, but I will accept that challenge."

Dr. Kyle replied, "Frankly, all science is based upon the logical application of appropriate tests to any proposition or theory about reality, in order to determine the validity or truth of that proposition or theory versus its falsehood. We must agree on this basic premise, or else as I stated, I have other valuable things to do."

Maybe Dr. Kyle was open to the evaluation of an uncommon event after all. I responded, "Now I feel like I have come to the right person. Based upon my more limited experience with mathematics and logic proofs, science classes, and some other research, I accept what you have stated. You indicate that you will help me apply logical understanding to what occurred during my scientific test in which the outcome included off-the-charts results. In addition, it indicates you will share in my conclusion that it is relevant to a rational understanding of the most powerful and important reality of our existence as humans on this earth."

Dr. Kyle said, "Okay, enough with the intrigue and mystery. Off the charts is one thing; otherworldly is another. You have my interest. We have an agreement regarding the rules for proceeding. Let's stick to rational analyses and avoid wasting time on nonsense and theories that cannot be examined logically.

"Actually, we have used most of the time that I allotted for this appointment. I think this is a good stopping point in our discussion. Let's pick it up in three days when I have some more time available. Let's start that meeting with a review of logic, science, and the scientific method. I think we will probably come to a fairly quick conclusion as to what was faulty with your experiment, and therefore its results have no further implication for the logical mind." "I will look forward to it, Doctor. But don't underestimate my experiment's validity, or the possibility that when we are done, your perception of known reality will have been greatly expanded to include things you never imagined. See you in three days," I concluded. I left with great anticipation for our next meeting.

Dr. Kyle's aversion to the phrase *otherworldly* had me a little concerned. But I chose to believe that he saw that description as applying to only physical life as we know it, existing on other physical worlds like other planets or something like that. Because of his aversion, I would try to avoid using that specific name again with him. He would learn, whether or not I used that specific descriptive phrase again, that I was talking about a world filled with life—some very powerful, beyond the physical world. Maybe *another dimension* was a better phrase than *otherworldly*. It was a world that included our physical world as a subset, yet the beings that existed there had abilities beyond the laws of the more limited physical world.

= 2 =

THE BOUNDARIES OF REALITY

And I know such a man—whether in the body or out of the body I do not know, God knows—how he was caught up into Paradise.

—2 Corinthians 12:3–4 (NKJV)

As I headed to Dr. Kyle's office, I attempted to prepare myself to hold back from jumping right into the extraordinary occurrences that I was going there to discuss and evaluate. It was going to be difficult to discipline my thoughts and conversation to strictly follow the scientific method of analyzing things. He was going to be one tough cookie. To him, the events already shared were outside the box. He had not even heard the mind-blowing conclusion to the Descartes experiment, as I called it. I decided to trust my own amateur knowledge of the flow of logic so I could discipline myself to follow his line of examination. Then possibly for the first time, I would, after all of these years, have someone with whom I could openly and completely share the experience that was very real yet challenged the world's currently accepted definition of reality.

While walking down the covered esplanade toward the math and science buildings on the university campus, I felt inspired by the breathtaking view of the ocean. As I momentarily stopped there, tingling with awe, I was stricken with the folly of atheism. To me, atheism boiled down to using one's own acknowledged intelligence to claim that intelligence cannot exist. It was far more logical that our world of reality included much more than the physical world, including a grand Designer, than to believe that objects like rocks and small bacteria, or even some of our physical body parts, somehow spontaneously generated intelligence and feelings. I realized that I had the very special advantage of having traveled outside the physical world, but even without that, it was obvious to me that the view-inspired tingling I was experiencing did not originate within physical objects that had no feelings. I found myself wondering how many people or other entities, alive in the nonphysical world that surrounds us, may be following along with me or simply passing by. Maybe some were hanging around just to watch the exchange with Dr. Kyle.

I could not help but think briefly about those of my friends and associates over the years, some of them very formally educated, who instead of exploring the boundaries of their intelligence and known reality had chosen to stand behind a mental fortress they had constructed out of oversimplified thoughts like "If I cannot see it or touch it, it is not real." These same people believe in mathematics, logic, intelligence, emotions, the laws of physics, fairness, good versus bad, the concept of infinite (e.g., the universe has no known boundary), and many more concepts they cannot see, touch, or explain. Yet they voluntarily chose to cut off thinking about certain things (unless of course they wanted to feed someone else's wealth by paying to see a science fiction movie for the sake of entertainment). How was it that so many could choose to believe in a plethora of certain things they could not see or touch, and yet they refused to consider the possible reality of other things they cannot see or touch? It seemed that evidence of the nonphysical world was a wind to which they had constructed a barricaded shelter in their minds.

I had never been one to immerse myself in a pool of half-measures, so I intended to take this exploration of logic with Dr. Kyle to the ultimate analysis of the boundaries of "reality"—the existence of God. Although some may think of that particular concept as a long shot regarding the application of logic, they had obviously not had an experience like the Descartes experiment. That experience taught me a simple rule about evaluating reality, namely that a truly logical and intelligent mind believing that man's science is ever expanding the boundaries of known reality cannot at the same time firmly believe that there are absolute immovable limits on the boundaries of that same known reality.

"Good morning, Glenn," Dr. Kyle greeted me. His mood seemed upbeat, and I was relieved, because the scientific evaluation of the topic at hand obviously required an open and clear mind ready to evaluate the facts. Logically, a mind cluttered with roadblocks of preconceived notions could only limit and impede the road of the scientific process. Even his long-sleeve white shirt and light tan slacks exuded a brighter atmosphere than I had sensed last time in his office. However, the green tie and the tan coat hanging on his dark wood coat and hat rack by the door implied he was dressed more for something formal than a lighter mood.

"Thank you for seeing me again. I'm anxious to establish the rules for examining the Descartes experiment. And yes, it is okay to record our meeting again. In fact, you can consider that I have given standing permission for recording any further meetings we may have on this subject."

"Well," Dr. Kyle explained, "the rules are actually quite simple. The scientific method is universally accepted as the system for testing any proposition or theory about reality. It begins with establishing the theory or concept to be tested. Then a logical test is established to apply to the theory. Then the results are logically evaluated and compared to known facts and laws of reality."

Oh, boy. It was looking like we would have to climb through a bunch of professorial hurdles regarding logic before we got to the facts of the otherworldly experience. I guessed if I wanted him to sit through my recalling of the experience, I had to be willing to sit through his intellectual discussion of logic.

"That does sound simple," I responded, "but I recall from my most memorable science teachers that when they let the students choose how to test a principal, there was sometimes significant debate over the best way to logically test something. Is there always a 'best test'?"

"Glenn, as you obviously recall from your science classes, there are quite often multiple tests accepted as logical to the scientific community to establish the truth or falsehood of a principal or theory."

"Okay, Doctor. Because scientists are continuously discovering new attributes of our reality, is it safe to say that all boundaries of all known reality have not yet been scientifically established?" This was my shot at expediting the conclusion of the logic discussion, but it kind of backfired.

"Very clever, Glenn. All boundaries of known reality cannot be claimed by anyone, including the most respected scientists, as having been scientifically established. However, that fact cannot be used to presume that some fantastic idea or concept is real. One of my favorite summary definitions of science can now be easily found in Wikipedia. Science is defined there as 'the systematic enterprise of gathering knowledge about the world and organizing and condensing that knowledge into testable laws and theories.' Their discussion goes on to say that the generally accepted standard process for conducting science has become the scientific method I described earlier."

"In my amateur reading about the scientific method, Dr. Kyle, I have learned that in addition to establishing a logical test of a theory or principal, the field of science actually holds the scientist responsible for first deciding or establishing what theories or principals are even testable or worth testing. Doesn't that mean that it is possible some theories or principals not accepted by the general scientific community are actually true, but no scientists have tried or been able to design a test of that theory or principal that is accepted by the scientific community?"

"That is obviously true, Glenn, and in fact the main reason we are still sitting here together is that you first explained to me your decision as a college student to test, utilizing the scientific method, the theory claimed by the world-renown philosopher Descartes that 'I think, therefore I am.' That is an excellent example of the first test of the scientific method. A theory or principal has to be testable, and frankly, in all of my studies completed to obtain my degrees, I have never heard nor conceived of a logical test that can be applied to that theory. Yet you came to me and set forth a very simple one.

"Please remember that I have articles to read, articles to write, papers to grade, and lectures to prepare. Yet I am making time to discuss this issue with you. Although I am concerned about where you were taking your story of your experiment, I am definitely intrigued with your starting point. And now after discussing the logic of the scientific process with you, I am more interested to hear you out.

"Let's go back to your starting point: devising a test for the theory 'I think, therefore I am.' I understand that at that time, you were a college student with a logic and math major who had taken some science classes. When you heard of Descartes's theory in philosophy class, you decided to devise a test to disprove it or possibly establish its validity. Here is where step one of the scientific method comes into play. Is this theory testable? Do I have the story correct so far?"

"Excellent memory. You are right on."

"Okay. Whether or not you knew it at that time, one of the well-established logical methods of choosing what theory to test is to conclude that the results of the test would definitely discount a theory of reality. In fact, most pure scientists will tell you that the scientific method is commonly used to disprove an idea, notion, or theory about a specific attribute of reality. Then after a thorough process of elimination, what is left not disproven after extensive testing, and also consistent with documented observations, is accepted as the current theory of reality regarding the subject at hand."

"Wait a minute, Dr. Kyle. I recall in many science classes that our experiments showed something to be true, not untrue."

"Your teachers and professors had limited time in those classes. Therefore, the experiments often utilized in the classroom atmosphere are ones that show the theory being tested actually working. If students were shown all of the experiments that had been done to narrow down a theory, those negative outcome experiments would have taken up all of the class time, and students would lose interest in science by the droves."

"Wait another minute. Are you saying that the logic of science is that we believe in theories that are not disproven yet, rather than theories that are proven to be true?" I thought I had something here.

"Don't get carried away, Glenn—or try to oversimplify things for that matter. I am saying that science is a logical system of studying attributes of our reality. Studying has produced some facts as indisputable, some presumed facts that were later disproven, and elimination of many theories. Therefore, science is ever evolving in its quest to establish more and more attributes of our reality, but by its own definition, science is not all-knowing and has not yet come close to establishing a comprehensive set of rules regarding the attributes of our world and universe.

My ability to focus on all of this dry talk of the scientific process was wearing thin. I felt a current of air movement and wondered whether some of those beings I had encountered while outside my body were hanging around in the room. If they were, I felt they would try to prod me to get the discussion to the exciting heart of the matter. I felt like Dr. Kyle was a giant covered in armor, guarding his heavily fortified city that he believed housed the known facts of the physical world. I imagined him seeing the little objects sailing right through him and the fortified walls of his Reality City as though on wings that could slice through his armor and fortifications. They were things like feelings, emotions, inspirations, insights, and intelligence. Even though he saw them breaching his armor and fortifications, and freely moving between the inside and outside of both him and his Reality City, he simply turned his back on them. It was as though to him, those things could exist outside his Known Reality City, but logic and science couldn't.

I kept this little summary vision to myself and continued listening, knowing that soon we would get to the actual occurrences and conclusions I had come there to discuss and analyze. It wasn't easy, but knowing that I was close to openly and rationally examining what was outside those "city walls" helped keep me focused, especially because I had traveled through those walls myself.

I focused on listening as he continued.

"Think about the theories of Isaac Newton. Many of his theories regarding the laws of the physical world were revolutionary at the time but became accepted as the facts of our reality. Then along came the theory of relativity. Then there was the concept and study of quantum physics. Now, many scientists are running tests to eliminate attributes of accepted Newtonian theories of our physical world laws, and then they have to establish a replacement theory. That replacement theory for a particular attribute of our reality is tested and tested, and when finally eliminated in part or in whole, our knowledge of reality is narrowed. The known attributes of our reality become a narrower and narrower set of attributes, and that narrowing is commonly called scientific advancement as we come closer and closer to knowing precisely an attribute of the reality of our existence."

"It sounds like science has a long way to go before everything about our world is adequately explained." I thought I was making a powerful statement here. After all, in this discussion, and with some prodding from me, Dr. Kyle had agreed that science was a process for discovering and/or eliminating theories about certain attributes of reality, and it was not a conclusive explanation of everything. However, without reaction to my self-perceived powerful comment, he continued.

"A prominent scientist named Richard Feynman left us all with a quote on this topic back in the sixties … Let me see if I can find it." He opened one of his desk drawers and picked out a sheet of paper. "Yes, it's right here; I refer to it quite often in my lectures. He described science as follows:

> The principle of science, the definition, almost, is the following—*The test of all knowledge is experiment.* Experiment is the *sole judge* of scientific truth. But

what is the source of knowledge? Where do the laws that are to be tested come from? Experiment, itself, helps to produce these laws, in the sense that it gives us hints. But also needed is imagination to create from these hints the great generalizations – to guess at the wonderful, simple, but very strange patterns beneath them all, and then to experiment to check again whether we have made the right guess.

"He also observed, 'There is an expanding frontier of ignorance … things must be learned only to be unlearned again or, more likely, to be corrected.' Now, with that in mind, let's get on with the subject at hand, which has interested me as possibly legitimately expanding the boundaries of known reality—your Descartes experiment."

"Fine, Dr. Kyle. However, I wonder how many citizens of the world, and more importantly, teachers of our children, are aware that not even the greatest of human minds have ever been able to establish the actual existence of any humanly comprehendible, absolute boundaries of the reality in which we all exist."

=3=

THE DESCARTES EXPERIMENT

The hand of the Lord came upon me and brought
me out in the Spirit.

—Ezekiel 37:1a (NKJV)

"So, Glenn, when you decided to test the Descartes proposition that
'I think, therefore I am,' you first dissected the logical components of
that statement. That is, that it describes a proposed action, thinking,
causing a result, existing. Then, as I recall from your story, you
decided that was a testable action-result relationship."

"Exactly. And the challenge was how to test it. My friend Ted
and I ..."

"You didn't mention anything about a friend. Glenn, my analysis
is worthless if I do not have all of the facts of the experiment. What
else did you leave out?"

Whoops. Confusing or irritating Dr. Kyle was the last thing
I wanted to do. "Sorry, Dr. Kyle. I didn't see his presence as that
relevant to the substance of what occurred. I was anxious to get
to the reality-challenging results of the experiment. I didn't leave
anything else out."

"I need you to tell me more about this person who evidently
shared this experience with you."

While clearly remembering that life-altering discussion during the walk that Ted and I shared from philosophy class back to the dorm that day so long ago, I explained, "Actually, Ted was my college roommate and a very good friend. He had been a high school athlete and was a high achiever who aced most of his courses. He and I shared an enthusiasm for intellectual challenges, and we happened to take the same philosophy course. Our course section met in the early afternoon, and it was the last class of the day for each of us. The professor, a past valedictorian at Cambridge, had challenged the class with a thought-provoking discussion of the famous Descartes quote, 'I think, therefore I am.' Ted and I were both fascinated with some of the ideas and comments generated, and we kept the discussion going as we walked across campus from the class back to our dorm room."

"So you and Ted embarked upon this venture together?"

"Well, yes, but it didn't turn out the same for each of us."

"Glenn, your friend's role seems relevant to me. Why do you think details of his involvement are irrelevant?"

"We did create and commence the experiment together. He also left his body, but it happened a little later for him, and in fact his entrance to the nonphysical world accompanied the eerie, scary, and thrilling encounter with some more powerful beings and events that resulted in my return to my body."

"More powerful beings?" Dr. Kyle queried. "I thought you were here to use logic in the analysis of the event. We have discussed the theory and process of logic as it is used to examine the validity of a proposition. Please remember that the facts are the cornerstones of the trail on the road map to a logical conclusion."

"I am absolutely committed to logical analysis. I am also committed to sharing the precise facts of the event exactly the way they occurred. Please remember that this was no ordinary, everyday experience. The reason I am here is because it was a life-altering experience." I hoped that this slip of the tongue in disclosing one of the major events that occurred later in the experience would not cost the interest or involvement of the skeptical Dr. Kyle.

"So what happened with Ted will be included in the complete recounting of what happened?"

"Yes," I assured him, relieved that he was still with me.

Dr. Kyle leaned back in his chair in a thoughtful pose, playing with a pen in his hands. "So while you and Ted debated how to test this theory, your amateur analysis as a student of math and logic was that the easiest test to first try would be to disprove the theory rather than prove it true. As we have already discussed, this is precisely the scientific method. The only scientific experiment ingredient missing is that proving the theory not true does not narrow down the possible causal relationships between thinking and existing. We all know that everyone breathing and thinking does exist."

"Listening to you causes me to wonder where this study could have gone if I hadn't been so shunned by the people around me at the time. I believe we came very close to proving that thinking thoughts of physical world things is directly related to physical world existence, and the elimination of physical world thoughts is directly related to—"

"Glenn," Dr. Kyle interrupted. He brought his chair forward and now leaned forward with his elbows resting on his perfectly organized, clean desk. "I am captivated, but I have to stay on my track of thinking in order to come to new conclusions, if I am indeed headed to new conclusions. You decided to test Descartes's theory by rejecting thoughts and waiting to see whether you still existed. Frankly, you must understand how absurd this sounds. I believe the people who refused to believe or listen to your test results back then were more rational than ignorant. I am seeing this story through, probably because you are now more studied in your presentation, and I am aware of some related issues that have developed in the scientific community since that time. In any event, please tell me again about 'rejecting thoughts.'"

"Ted and I sat on the edge of our respective dorm room beds and agreed to close our eyes and attempt to reject thoughts by choosing to not know the name for things that came to our minds. After a few minutes, we both opened our eyes and discussed our experience. We agreed that sensations around us were interfering with our efforts. For example, suddenly realizing your back is tired from sitting up straight interferes with a 100 percent focus on the mental exercise.

"After a while, we chose to go to opposite corners of the room and get into a sitting fetal position to resume our efforts to reject thoughts. This position seemed to provide a better atmosphere for conducting the experiment as the focus of my mind became sharper. Soon I was able to isolate various physical objects in my mind's eye against a background that seemed as empty and dark as the void of deep space. First a chair stood all by itself in my mind's view with many other more vague objects floating around within view. Then as I focused on the chair and attempted to let go of my knowledge of what it was called (reject the thought), it began moving toward me, and at the moment I felt I had convinced myself I did not know its name, it whisked past my face and disappeared behind me. Then a pillow came into focus and sat there in my mind's view as I worked on convincing myself I did not know what to call it. Finally, as I let go of the knowledge of the name of the pillow, it too moved past me out of view."

"So your devised system of rejecting thoughts consisted of picturing an object and convincing yourself that you didn't know what to call it?" Dr. Kyle asked while still leaning forward.

"Yes, exactly," I answered. "This process continued, and with each object that appeared, the time was shorter between its appearance and its whisking out of view past me. As this process sped up, I vividly recall that beginning with a light bulb, several objects began to concurrently show themselves and then get in line behind one another in my mind's view. The entire line first crawled but then moved faster and faster toward my face and out of the space in front of me. I was transfixed and suddenly realized that I had gone from controlling the situation to helplessly watching it unfold. I didn't know why the line of objects was moving faster and faster, but I was keenly aware they were headed directly for my nose instead of past me like the previous single objects. Then as I stared into the accelerating light bulb and braced for impact, I suddenly lost the thought of its name, and it veered to the right and zoomed past my right ear and out of view."

I paused when Dr. Kyle leaned back again, farther than before. "Go on," he said.

"The compass became unnamed and veered at the last minute past my left ear. The measuring scale and a seemingly unending line of objects kept coming at my face faster and faster, with each object at the last second losing its name and veering past the opposite ear as the previous object."

"Are you saying each object very specifically moved past your face on the opposite side as the immediately preceding object?" Dr. Kyle interrupted.

"Yes. I can still see the last object as clearly as that day all of those years ago. It was a simple wall mount light switch. As it just missed my nose and sped past my right ear, there was only empty space left in my mind's view. However, this is where the truly phenomenal occurred."

"So you didn't yet see this as something phenomenal at this stage?"

"I see your point," I said with a smile. "I am speaking with the advantage of knowing the whole story, and it goes far beyond the moving objects in my mind's eye. After the last one, the light switch, I saw only the empty, dark space of my mind's eye for a second. Then before I had time to think about it, I found myself not in my mind's eye at all but my actual self, hovering in the air near the ceiling of the dorm room, looking at my very real surroundings in broad daylight."

With a wry grin, Dr. Kyle said, "Now we are getting somewhere. I'm glad you described the broad daylight so I can picture the situation. What drugs were involved?"

"Like I mentioned to you previously, there were no drugs of any kind involved. This was two college students who enjoyed intellectual challenges, conducting a clear-headed experiment right after philosophy class in the afternoon."

"I believe my curiosity about drug involvement is very logical. Okay, so you were hovering, as you describe it. What sensations did you experience?"

"There was no sensation of temperature or other physical world sensations, nor any sense of physical world limitations. I did have feelings like fascination, for example, and I could see physical world things. As I scanned the room, I saw somebody sitting in the fetal position on the floor in the corner of the room. My fascination turned first to shock and then to exhilaration as I realized I was looking down at the back of my own head, and my body was still sitting there. Then—"

The sound of something pounding on the door interrupted me. "What's that?"

"I'm sorry, Glenn. That's the dean knocking. He's here to go with me to the faculty meeting, where I'm scheduled to make a presentation. As I said, your story is very captivating, but I am going to have to take a step back in considering the investment of my professional time with you regarding this. I do think we have covered the application of science and logic agreeably today, but I am concerned right now with the relationship between the application of science and logic and your story. Specifically, I am concerned about the part of the scientific method that requires there to be observable phenomena or patterns of behavior consistent with, or opposite to, the phenomena or pattern of behavior being tested. I will give some thought to whether I am so interested in your fantastic story out of my desire for entertainment, or whether there is a genuine professional element to my interest. I will call you if I want to pursue this further with you."

As I walked back to the car, the ocean seemed farther away. The brightness of the world around me had darkened. The weight of the air felt heavier. Were the people from the other dimensions laughing at me, or discouraged with me? For that matter, were they even paying attention? Maybe I was simply experiencing the disappointment common to humans that results from lack of patience. After all, from what I knew of the nonphysical world, time was not the same there.

Days passed while waiting for his call. I began the process of settling in once again for the disappointment of having my very real and exceptional experience blown off.

Then a few weeks later, the call came.

= 4 =

NOT ALONE

We are confident, yes, well pleased rather to be absent from the body and to be present with the Lord.

—2 Corinthians 5:8 (NKJV)

"Glenn, I invited you back today because I did a little research regarding the out-of-body experience to which you're claiming your Descartes experiment took you. Previous to your visits, I had heard about such things, but frankly I dismissed them as people ignoring reality and creating a fantastic story to get attention. I never considered this topic relevant to scientific study and advancement of the parameters of our known world. However, you have impressed me as a fairly normal, thoughtful, and rational person, which gave your story enough credibility for me to at least do a little independent research on the topic."

I said, "I'm glad to hear that from you. In the many years since my experience, I've gone from initially feeling extremely lonely because no one around me believed any part of it to jumping out of my chair one night when the old show *In Search Of* did a segment on the topic, to reading about others' experiences when the computer age finally made so much information from all over the world easily accessible to everyone. I know that today there is related information on line under topics like out-of-body experience (OBE), astral projection, spirit walking, near-death experience (NDE), and probably many more. I recall reading about a cardiologist from the Netherlands named Pim van Lommel who gathered documentation and testimony regarding NDEs. Just a second—let me get my notes on this from my wallet."

"You carry around notes on this in your wallet?"

"Yes. Although I am glad to have you with your calm, analytic demeanor to discuss this with, I guarantee that until you have such an experience as I did, you cannot fully grasp the impact on one's life and perception of reality. More important, I cherish credibility. And it has seemed that credibility to most people does not exactly go hand in hand with this experience. Here it is—Pim van Lommel did a clinical study of cardiac arrest patients. Sixty-two of the 344 patients in the study who were resuscitated were documented to have had out-of-body experiences while their bodies were clinically dead with flat-lined brain stem activity. They described hovering in the room and recounted specific events in detail, including conversations between people in the room while their body was clinically dead."

"Do you consider it some sort of religious experience?"

"Interesting question, Dr. Kyle." Considering that my experience was clearly beyond the day-to-day realities of the physical world, I always found it fascinating that those folks I knew who claimed that they were religious were some of the biggest critics and naysayers. This group, by definition, believed in a supernatural spiritual world. Many of them operated on an intelligent and rational acceptance that God and the spiritual world were beyond their complete understanding. However, far too many of them operated on the "God in a box" syndrome. It was these folks who took strong stands that I either didn't really have this experience or that it was of Satan because it didn't fit into their box of knowledge of a world that they, by their own definition, could not completely comprehend.

"Let's talk about that later, after you've heard everything that actually happened to me. Remember, your dean showed up for your meeting, and you cut off the recounting of my experience right when I left my body."

"Very well. I was about to explain that I did read about van Lommel's study, as well as much of the other literature in categories like the ones you mentioned. I also found references to a CIA project where they were conducting trials of having people leave their bodies in a controlled manner, 'float' out of a closed room and into another closed room, read or see something prepared for them to see in the second room, return to the first room, reenter their bodies, and explain what was in the second room."

"That is exactly what they were doing in that television show *In Search Of* all those years ago, Dr. Kyle!"

"Well, current references to that experiment seem sparse. I assume it was too difficult to control the out-of-body venture, or it simply wasn't real, or even possibly that it worked, in which case I can understand the CIA keeping it secret." He grinned.

"Does this mean we have established that there are sufficient existing observed phenomena so that my experiment has to be generally accepted as 'scientific'?"

"Don't get too carried away, Glenn. What I have read elsewhere and heard from you leads me to believe that there is sufficient observed phenomena to consider your experiment part of an overall approach to establish some properties of our reality that are in question and not yet proved one way or the other."

"I have attempted a logical general categorization of the information, so I could look for any relationships we could logically identify. I concluded that there are basically three groups of people. First, there are those who claim to have had a truly out-of-body experience where their essence was separated from their physical body. Second, there seems to be a group of people who have had some sort of quasidream state experience where their bodies were asleep, but they had a mental awareness experience that was more than a dream. Third, there are the people who have had no experience of any such kind."

I said, "I'm happy that you are taking this seriously. For whatever it is worth to your analysis, this happened in broad daylight during a fully clear-minded and conscious endeavor. There was no sleeping or dreaming, and I was separated from my body. I'd like to finish telling you what happened and where I went."

"Okay, have at it."

5

SENT BACK

And the man who journeyed with him stood
speechless, hearing a voice, but seeing no one.

—Acts 9:7 (NKJV)

"After studying the back of my body's head—which, trust me, is
more fascinating than one might think—I took off to explore."

"Whoa, whoa, Glenn. As I recall, you said you were seeing things
in your mind's eye, and then you found yourself outside your body.
Try again to explain the difference before getting into the taking off."

"My mind's eye only applies to the initial steps of the experiment,
and it means something I believe virtually everyone easily
understands. I was in my body with my eyes closed, but I was awake,
so my thoughts were visualizations. Just like the person who goes
to sleep by first closing his eyes and visualizing a peaceful scene to
become relaxed, or by counting visualized sheep, so he can go to
sleep. This may be a distinction one has to experience to completely
understand, but being outside the body is thoroughly unlike and
distinct from visualization while one's eyes are closed. During
visualization, no matter how excited or thrilling one's thoughts
may become, one still has a sense of being comfortably centered
within one's physical body and 'looking outward' at whatever one is

27

visualizing. The out-of-body experience is nothing like visualization. The description 'out of body' is an attempt to describe the fact that one's self or essence is specifically located or centered outside the physical body. During my experience, there was no confusion, doubt, or interpretation of sensations that can be described in any way other than I—what I consist of other than physical body parts—was clearly located in a specific location independent of the location of my physical body. I even knew the relative size and shape of my essence or self, but it is not describable in physical world terms.

"The out-of-body experience is also completely distinct from normal dreaming while asleep. Sometimes people have very vivid dreams where they believe they were really located in the setting of their dream due to the sensations they wake up with. However, dreaming is an exercise of the mind wherein one's body is visualized as in another location separate from the bed in which the actual body is sleeping. One also wakes up from sleeping. Again, during my experience, I did not go to sleep, visualize my body being somewhere else, or wake up from sleep. I simply exited from my physical body in broad daylight while wide awake."

"You understand, Glenn, that if what you are saying is true, this could have major implications about reality as we generally know and accept it.'

"I assume by *we*, you mean the people who believe there is no life outside the physical world experience. And yes, that is why I have come to a professor of logic to discuss it."

"Okay, I want to get back to the logical approach of your Descartes experiment, but for now why don't you finish telling me the rest of what happened first?"

"As I mentioned, I was hovering in the upper portion of the dorm room."

"Hold on, Glenn. Let's get some clarifications here. First, you said *I* describing the hovering. Were there not two of you—one 'essence' seemingly hovering, and one physical body in another location?"

"I can absolutely confirm that the only *me* that I had any

awareness of was the *me* that was hovering and without physical form."

"Interesting, and kind of spooky to the logical mind. Anyway, what exactly do you mean by hovering?"

"I don't know of any words that come close to describing attributes of that state of existence. Until I learn of any such words, I have only physical-world words at my disposal to use, and *hovering* is the best word I can think of right now. Maybe it would help define the experience more clearly if I used additional physical world words to describe additional attributes of that existence."

"Please do."

"I had no physical sensations even though I could see physical world things in their entirety. I had no sense of weight, or touch, or smell. These are things I realized immediately when I left my body. From the events that followed, I can tell you that there were absolutely no physical-world rules restricting my movement or perception in any way. The only physical world or human attribute I had was the ability to see the physical world around me even though I had no eyes as we humans know them. So *hovering* means I was in a certain location relative to the physical world, observing the world around me, and that initial specific location was in the air in the upper half of the dorm room. I was effortlessly maintaining that position and observing."

"Were you, in your nonphysical form, the only thing you were aware of other than the physical world items you were observing?"

"Great question, Dr. Kyle. You're the first of the people I have shared this experience with to ask that specific question. As I effortlessly hovered there, I was keenly aware of an entire world of existence beyond the physical items in my view. The physical world, including the bodies, items, and structures, as well as all of the rules of their interaction, were merely a subset of the world of which I now was a part. As I have stated, I was in a location describable in physical world terms. However, my shape, my consistency, my sensations, and my movement were not in the slightest way governed by physical world laws of particle interaction or motion. I was completely independent of all of the laws of physical science that I had studied in school, but at the same time I had sight and awareness of the physical world that was now a subset of the world I knew, and I still had all of my nonphysically oriented feelings."

With a hardy laugh, Dr. Kyle responded, "This sounds straight out of a science fiction movie about the nth dimension. Anyway, you've done a good job describing how nonphysical this world was, but because I have come this far with you, I would like to hear more about what else was with you in your nonphysical world dimension. Even more, I guess I am now in for the rest of the story, so let's give this new dimension a name so you can save some time in your descriptions. Let's call it the new dimension."

"A name is okay with me, but I find myself uncomfortable with many names for this existence because the names are self-limiting in their definition, and by using them, the experience is diminished from what really happened. Let's call it expanded reality. You see, it is a world that includes the physical world; it simply has more to it than the physical world. You could say the physical world is a subset of this expanded reality."

"Very well, Glenn, let's call it expanded reality. Now, go ahead and tell me more about it."

"Upon recognizing that I was separate from my physical body, I immediately sensed that the rules of the physical world did not apply to me. Shortly after sizing up my situation, I began to move around and went easily through the wall into the next dorm room. Then the next and so on, until I finally decided to go outside the dorm building and watch the people walking and driving in the area."

"Wow, Glenn. I have to admit you really have me going now. I want to know what you saw in the dorm rooms, what sensations you had, how far you could see outside, who out there was like you, and more. I don't know how much is curiosity and how much is scientific investigation. Unfortunately, I have to go right now. Maybe before I completely buy into this, I will try to have my own OBE and see what happens …"

"No," I immediately blurted out, getting emotional. "Don't do that."

"What elicited that reaction, Glenn? You seem genuinely concerned that I not even try."

"You have no road map for getting back into your body."

"Interesting. Are you saying it is not as simple as 'I want back now'?"

"I don't have instructions or a procedure that I know accomplishes that."

"Then how did you get back into your body? Or did I just find the hole in your fabricated story?"

"I was sent back. I didn't control it."

"So there was someone else in this expanded reality with you?"

"Yes. Multiple beings with different levels of ability, and different types of intentions."

"Wow. Okay, Glenn. Can you come back tomorrow afternoon?"

"I thought you had appointments on Tuesday afternoons."

"I'm going to cancel them if you can come in then."

"I'll be here."

I couldn't believe Dr. Kyle was considering trying to follow my story and attempt a planned OBE. I hoped he would follow my advice not to try. I also expect that after he slept on it, he would come in ready to beat the whole thing up with logical analysis.

=6=

SUPERNATURAL LOGIC

> While we are at home in the body we are absent
> from the Lord.
>
> —2 Corinthians 5:6 (NKJV)

As I stood waiting outside Dr. Kyle's office, I found myself once again wondering what disembodied personalities may be floating around, and whether they considered the ocean as beautiful as I did. Dr. Kyle had never been late. I wondered if he had gone ahead and tried the OBE. I hoped not because I'd meant what I'd said about not knowing a plan for getting back into his body. Worse yet, I hadn't told him the part about the extremely sinister forces out there.

He either followed my advice or found the secret for getting back, because he soon arrived. Even though he had gone back to darker clothes that I knew would cast that ominous sense of dominance over the air in his dark office, I was optimistic because he smiled when he saw me and seemed happy. Besides, I had dressed in my orange, green, and brown Hawaiian shirt, with tan cargo shorts, brown Rockport loafers, and subankle socks. How could the mood turn dark with that happy-go-lucky spring beach wear in the room?

"Hi, Glenn. Let's go inside."

As we walked through the door, I felt a chill. Was there an

interested gathering of nonphysical world participants coming through the door with us, or was that my imagination?

He started with, "Glenn, I listened to the recordings I made of our other meetings, and I want to pick up on the scientific logic of making conclusions about your experience."

Here we go again. I needed to work at staying calm and focused. This was as close as I had ever come to getting an atheistic, and a skeptically trained scientist and logician, to listen to the story and reasoning of my experience.

Dr. Kyle continued. "We have agreed that the scientific process includes starting with a theory about a portion or rule of our reality, then devising an experiment that, when concluded, can either rule out the theory or confirm the theory. Further, we agreed that many years ago, you devised an experiment to test Descartes's theory that we think, therefore we are. You attempted to 'not think' and see whether you still existed. Based upon the outcome, you could see whether any relationship between thinking and existing could be established. You then took me through your experiment to a point where 'rejecting thoughts' resulted in you departing from your physical body. Are we on the same page so far?"

"Pretty much, except that I don't want to leave out three clarifications. First, we also agreed that science as we know it is a process that humans have established for evaluating their known or observed world, and that the entirety of the boundaries of reality in which humans live has not even come close to being established through the human devised scientific process. Second, humans have generally acknowledged that there are many attributes of their reality and behavior patterns that they see and know exist, yet they cannot 'scientifically' establish their derivation—things like emotions and inspirations. Third, there are other known facts that humans observe and have titles for yet, with all of their logical scientific process, cannot adequately convert to humanly understandable concepts— things like infinity, where the physical universe begins and ends, where time begins and ends, et cetera."

"Like I have said before, for an amateur, you have put some real thinking and logic into your positions, Glenn. And yes, it is true that man, through his scientific process, has not yet established all of the boundaries of reality."

"Well, although I have not done all of the formal coursework to obtain doctorates, I have had the experience we have been talking about that has driven a lot of research and thought on my part."

"Back to the immediate point. What conclusions about reality do you think your experiment brought you to?"

"First of all, Descartes was wrong. I experienced the fact that I exist in a world where the physical world is just a subset. While being present strictly in that world and not limited by residing in our human physical world body, our abilities and comprehensions (that is, thinking capacity) far exceed those of the physical world limited human capability. Therefore, I believe it is logical to conclude that as humans, we—that is, our essence, or our soul—are in existence prior to our ability to think as humans think.

"Wow, Glenn, isn't that a bit of a leap? After all, maybe Descartes had knowledge of an expanded dimension of existence, and he was including that in his conclusion."

My immediate thought at this point was more that Dr. Kyle was allowing the whole expanded reality dimension while offering his critique and question. Maybe he was warming up to the conclusion of the expanded reality?

I answered, "Descartes made no mention of anything other than a strictly physical-world human existence in this quote, nor any other of his quotes that I could find. Therefore, I believe I have been logical in concluding that his theories and philosophies are based strictly on the realities of the physical world. He was saying that humans exist as humans because they can think thoughts from and pertinent to their physical world. Furthermore, because I traveled to the expanded reality where I definitely existed, using the specific conduit of rejecting human or physical world thoughts, then I am before I think."

"Not bad, Glenn. However, you are basing your conclusion on

the fact that Descartes meant something certain when he delivered his famous quote, which we can't absolutely know for sure."

"Thank you for pointing this out. It doesn't change my conclusion, but I can restate it: We exist in the form of a soul or essence, prior to inhabiting a human body, and we are (exist), therefore we think (human-based, physical-world thoughts)."

"Okay, let's say I accept that logic and your conclusion regarding Descartes's quote. There still remains your conclusion of existing outside the human body and world. That seems like a larger topic than Descartes's correctness."

"Remember our discussion about how sometimes researchers find a bonus discovery about reality when investigating another?"

He nodded and gestured to go on.

"Well, even though I consider that proving Descartes wrong is a pretty big deal, that is nothing compared to what else I learned during that experiment. Based upon what happened during that experiment, it takes no leap of faith to accept the truth of God's existence."

"It seems you have chosen your words in an attempt to make the leap of faith required to believe in God—while trying to claim it's not actually a leap of faith at all. Let me remind you that the definition of science is centered upon the concept of testing theories of observed phenomena."

"Dr. Kyle, you wanted to hear more of the details of my out-of-body experience, and maybe we should go through some of that before getting too deep into the 'God's existence' discussion."

"Glenn, the problem I see right now is that I need to believe we are on the track of something relevant to the use of the scientific process, or I cannot allocate the time necessary to sit through any more of it. If this whole thing is leading to the idea that we should throw science out the window and use our imagination to color and expand the thought process to some grand, improvable conclusion about the existence of God, I'd rather be reading fiction for entertainment."

I hoped bringing up God hadn't blown this whole discourse. I guessed that if it ended here, at least by finally reaching out and pursuing this discourse with someone, I had finally found a relief valve for my pent-up desire to share the otherworldly but very real experience I had lived through. On the other hand, I was not going to stop. He would have to throw me out. After having been in the expanded reality that included much, much more than the physical world, I knew that we existed independent of our bodies. I also could confirm that God was active in that expanded reality dimension. Knowing that skeptics had a hard enough time accepting the expanded reality, let alone meeting God there, I had examined the existence of God from a logical perspective, and I came to the conclusion that not only the existence of God but the relevance of God was paramount to the human experience. It seemed, however, that I had hit a nerve with Dr. Kyle. As I gathered my thoughts in order to attempt to keep the interest of the esteemed logic professor in evaluating my conclusions, I would have to be careful. I sensed that it was too late to go back to the details of the OBE, because he would be distracted by the knowledge that I was headed to conclusions he currently felt he could never accept.

I replied, "Dr. Kyle, I didn't mean to make it sound that I was jumping off of the logical track. I would like to make a couple of observations in an effort to show that I am trying to think logically, and I request your assistance in staying on track."

"Go ahead."

"Okay, at one time, all of the greatest human minds thought the earth was flat."

"Glenn," Dr. Kyle interrupted. "Please don't insult me with the obvious. When I say go ahead, I am expecting an intellectually challenging discussion worth my time."

Whoops. I guessed that was the wrong track to proceed with. I'd try another. "I think it is very important to examine conclusions that are the general consensus of the scientists that are not believers in God, Dr. Kyle. Maybe you can help me with a more up-to-date review. For many decades, this group of scientists believed that the physical universe was infinite and had always existed. I believe I have read that the general consensus of this group regarding the origin of the universe is now the big bang theory, a theory that some sort of spontaneous eruption of forces, and creation of matter, brought the physical universe into existence, and it is expanding outward."

"Glenn," he interrupted, "that is correct. However, I have to know where you are going with this. We are supposed to be examining the results of your experiment regarding Descartes's statement that we think, and therefore we are. Then you suddenly change tracks to something about God's existence. I didn't pursue this investigation with you so that we could jump off the logic track into a philosophical or theological discussion of improvable theories."

"Leaving my body, traveling around, and having supernatural interactions is not exactly the everyday experience of the science lab. I am here to ask you to apply your talent, knowledge, and experience in the field of logic to examine that occurrence. The fact that it is an 'outside the box' occurrence means that we need to be pressing the limits of logic, not just applying logic as though we were in the classroom examining the textbook or 'inside the box' problems."

The silence was deafening as we sat staring at each other. I sensed he was controlling his emotions and giving thought to my words. I didn't want to interrupt his thoughts, but neither could I look away. I had to make him understand that I was very serious about both my experience and his examination of it. It made me uncomfortable that he seemed so calm while sitting there staring at me. Finally, he spoke.

"So why did you jump from the details of your experience to the concept of God?"

I took a breath. Even though his words were laced with skepticism, he was still discussing my comments instead of throwing me out. I responded, "First, I want to say that your challenging questions are helping me keep my thoughts on a logical plane, even if it may not seem that way to you right now."

"Okay, let's go on."

He was something else, cold and precise. I was tempted to scrap the whole thing and find someone else to present this experience to. I glanced out the window to the ocean, hoping for inspiration. When I turned back toward him, he sat there like he owned the ocean, and that was when it hit me. His tough-mindedness and precision thinking was exactly my inspiration. The greater the challenge, the greater value in each successful step of its pursuit.

I proceeded. "Dr. Kyle, there are two reasons that I brought up the subject of God. First of all, as a parallel ratio comparison: God is to man's science as my experience outside my body is to man's everyday experiences. Second, a potential direct comparison: once it is established that life exists independent of the physical world, then the odds that God's existence is logical increase exponentially."

"Not bad, Glenn. However, we have already had the discussion that science is not a thing versus some other thing. It is simply a process. The strongest component of that process is logic. Therefore, science is not limited like you made it sound. The scientific process can be extended to other things or phenomena through the use of logic."

"That is why I came to see you. Dr. Kyle, you have made it known that you are an atheist. Maybe when I compared God to man's science earlier, I really meant an atheist' science."

"That's fair. You've used some pretty decent logic to introduce the possible existence of God into our discussions, so we can allow it. However, I think I need to hear the details of the remainder of your experience before the logic or nonlogic of God's existence becomes relevant. Your conclusion that rejecting thoughts of physical-world things can take you to a nonphysical world is very intriguing and, I must say, somewhat scientifically logical. However, it seems premature to jump to the conclusion that God exists."

=7=

THE BIG BANG THEORY

Now when He had spoken these things, while they
watched, He was taken up, and a cloud received Him
out of their sight.

—Acts 1:9 (NKJV)

I said, "You may be right that I should finish sharing the details
of my expanded reality, or supernatural experience, before we can
complete a logical discussion regarding God's existence. However,
before I go on, I want to throw out a logical challenge to the obvious
presumption of your last statement."

"What are you talking about, Glenn?"

"Doctor, why do you believe it is more logical to believe that a
living God does not exist than the fact that a living God does exist?"

"That's easy …" He paused and sat there thinking. I found myself
on the edge of my seat, waiting.

"Glenn," he continued, "logic, which is the thread of all science,
has to have some sort of pattern of observed events or particle
interactions in order to draw a logical conclusion about a portion of
our reality. The concept of God is a theory with no observed events
or interactions to logically examine."

"I guess you have decided to discount the stories of acts and events described in the Old and New Testaments of the Jewish and Christian Bibles, wherein the occurrences were outside the rules of the physical world?"

"Glenn, please don't go there. I believe the people who want to believe those stories and accounts will believe them, and that it is just as possible to find some principal of the physical world to explain them."

"What about the logical scientific system of putting forth a theory that matches observed phenomena, then running various tests to hopefully narrow down the possible conclusions?"

"That is proper science. What does it have to do with God's existence?"

"Well, one example, which we briefly discussed earlier, is that the scientific community that has been studying the observed facts regarding the physical universe has generally come to the logical conclusion that the physical universe came into existence through a singular event that they have labeled the big bang."

"Glenn, a scientific conclusion of a single event of physical world creation does not equate to God's existence."

"I understand. However, I believe that logically, the observation made of a singular creation event makes it relevant to examine more closely the concept of an intelligent creator of the physical universe."

"Did I miss something, or are you starting to talk in circles?"

"Actually, I meant something much simpler than it sounded. If the entire physical universe originated from some sort of big bang, which is more logical?"

1. The spontaneous big bang originated from some sort of unexplainable interaction of components that actually did not yet exist.
2. A superhuman, nonphysical intelligent being existed and created the entire physical universe as a subset of its nonphysical world dominion.

There was silence ... followed by more silence.

Then he spoke. "Glenn, I've always had a quick and easy response for that question until today. I have simply discounted any possibility of a superhuman, nonphysical being. As I start to answer you, my mind is evaluating your still unfinished story of your OBE, where I think you were about to explain that you encountered another being. Also, I have to consider the many other articles I have now read about OBEs and NDEs. We've taken it this far. Let's hear about the rest of your experience, and then we can talk about any conclusions that seem appropriate."

"Well, okay, but let's make a commitment to hear out the whole experience."

"Are you suggesting that I'm going to stop you?" he asked.

"I simply have the advantage of knowing whom I met, and what I encountered, when outside of my body."

"Okay, okay. Finish it. As I recall, you were floating around as a nonphysical being, traveling through physical structures like walls, and there was another being there. I do have one question before you continue. You were a young man, and you mentioned traveling through the dorms. Did you search out anything that would be considered sexually stimulating?" He completed his question with a grin.

"Before I move on, I will clear up two concepts you mentioned. First, there were multiple live beings in that expanded, nonphysical world. Second, I did see things that some humans would consider sexually stimulating. However, this is probably the best example to use to clarify my earlier explanation that I had no physical-world sensations. Don't get me wrong. I was experiencing indescribable exhilaration. It simply wasn't physically oriented or stimulated. The exhilaration was more a consequence of being free from the boundaries of the physical world. I was in a spirit form and not influenced by the young man's physical body that I had left behind. The sight of a sexy girl, for example, was no different than seeing a car drive by, or any other physical object for that matter, none of which had any particular impact upon me. I guess I would amend that by saying I had an awareness of the living soul within each physical human regardless of physical gender or attractiveness."

"Interesting. What about the multiple beings?"

"First, I want to complete the description of my motion. I have said that I could travel through walls and physical barriers. That's true, but it's not the whole story. It describes only my movements in kind of a physical-world manner—as in moving from one physical location to another."

"How else can you move other than from one place to another?"

"I found that I could think of a physical world place and then be there."

"Are you certain that you didn't get this teleporting idea from science fiction movies?"

"Absolutely. I am telling you exactly what happened in that very real experience. I realize that changing location via thought has been explored in the movies and literature. What I can confirm for you is that those original writers of this travel concept either imagined it or else had a similar experience to my OBE before ever first writing about it. You and I both know that people describing this type of experience prior to very recently would have jeopardized their reputations and careers, and therefore we'll never know whether they had this experience or not before writing it up as fiction."

"Well, how far did you travel in that manner?"

"Keep in mind that I was part of a world that exists beyond the limits of the physical world, so describing distances and locations is simply not the same as using a map of the physical world. Although I came to understand there were no physical-world limitations on my movements, I was in that state for a relatively short while. I can tell you that I 'jumped' from building to building, and to locations across the campus, and into the streets simply via a thought to do so.

"So you moved around by 'jumping' instead of continuous motion?"

"Not instead of. Again, my motion was a different kind of motion than exists within the physical world. Relative to the physical world, I guess you could describe my motions as either continuous or jumping. I could simply move at will in a manner that can only be understood in that expanded reality world.

"In fact, the end of this experience became accelerated when I perceived that my friend had left his body and entered that world as well. When that happened, I was exploring around, but upon perceiving his presence, I was drawn to him and immediately found myself back in our dorm room, where he was 'hovering' above his physical body."

"Why was that the end of the experience?"

"It wasn't the end. It was simply the first in a series of events that led to the end. There were basically two portions to the experience. First, I was exploring and experiencing a state of exhilaration. With the arrival of Ted, things changed. When I arrived in proximity of him, bringing with me my sense of exhilaration, I sensed in him more of a feeling of trepidation."

"Then I saw it."

"With your nonexistent eyes?" Dr. Kyle asked with a smirk on his face. "What did you see?"

I continued without responding to him. I decided he was simply having a little fun, because I had already explained seeing in that dimension. "The dark force approaching him."

"Come on, Glenn. The 'dark force'? Was it a force, a nonphysical being, or Darth Vader?"

"I thought describing it more clearly would put you off, but obviously using a somewhat vague description was worse than simply saying what or who it was."

"That's true. But I'm also getting a little edgy because I am running late to start preparing for another meeting, and I'm anxious to get to the end of the story of your experience. Sorry for the sarcasm. Let's set next Tuesday at 2:00 to try to wrap it up."

It seemed like a good time to me to leave him with some thoughts regarding the "existence of God" issue. I hoped he wouldn't get irritated about it. "Not a problem," I said. "Before going, I would like to leave you with a list of quotes from some scientists that I have with me."

"Okay."

I handed him the list of quotes.

I didn't know whether he was in a hurry or actually considering a thoughtful discussion about the existence of God. As I walked toward the parking lot and watched the bright sun's glimmer reflect off of the ocean, I felt elevated by that brightness, like it was lifting me to a new, brighter future. I already knew my ultimate destiny. Was I being too emotional over the hope that Dr. Kyle would abandon his atheism? Hope was a good and positive thing. Maybe the positive emotion was simply a good and perfectly normal experience for the circumstance.

=8=

SCIENCE DEMANDS A CREATOR

> Whether in the body I do not know, or whether out
> of the body I do not know, god knows – such a one
> was caught up to the third heaven.
>
> —2 Corinthians 12:2 (NKJV)

The following is what I handed to Dr. Kyle, along with my brief
overview at the end.

Some people didn't want to hear my story because, as they said,
they'd rather follow what scientists say than a story that can't be
proven. That fact has caused me to read the writings and statements
of several scientists over the years. What I discovered is that all
scientists are not atheists. In fact, there are many more than one
might think whose scientific research has convinced them that there
is in fact an intelligent Creator of the physical world that they study
in their respective fields. There are even more who acknowledge that
Darwin's evolution theory doesn't work, but they continue to grope
for atheistic theories because of their non-scientific-based refusal to
believe there is a God. Among many individual writings and articles,

I came across two authors who each have written a book that is a resource of quotes and work summaries from multiple scientists. One was written by a journalist with a law degree who set out to interview scientists with the purpose of concluding that the atheists are correct and there is no real support for a Creator. The result of his interviews was that he became a believer and discounts atheism. The other is a respected scientist in multiple fields with his doctorate in physical chemistry who has written many technical articles, as well as the book referenced later.

The first author is Lee Strobel. The result of his research and interviews is that he became a believer in an intelligent Creator and wrote a book called *The Case for a Creator* (Zondervan, 2004). In that book, he summarizes the observations of several scientists and has made research of this nature much simpler for the rest of us. He interviews major players from virtually every major scientific field, and he also relays some quotes he learned about in his research. Topics covered include what was wrong with some of the factors in Darwin's experiment and the logical conclusion of the existence of an intelligent Creator. It's definitely impossible to grasp the complete and very powerful value of Mr. Strobel's book without reading it in its entirety. I strongly recommend this book. However, instead of expecting someone so busy to read that entire book during the course of our discussions, I have produced a few quotes from it. These particular quotes, though not even scratching the surface of the book's full content or the rich volume of scientists' quotes, do provide some powerful logic for the existence of God.

Allan Rex Sandage, PhD, 1926–2010. Doctorate from Cal Tech. Renowned cosmologist who has done groundbreaking work with quasars, globular clusters, stars, and galaxy locations. He spent some time working as an assistant to Edwin Hubble. He has been honored by the American Astronomical Society, the Swiss Physical Society, the Royal Astronomical Society, and the Swedish Academy of Sciences, receiving astronomy's equivalent of the Nobel Prize. He became a Christian in 1983.

It was my science that drove me to the conclusion that the world is much more than can be explained by science. It was only through the supernatural that I can understand the mystery of existence. (70)

Stephen C Meyer, PhD, b. 1958. Doctorate from Cambridge. Degrees and studies: philosophy, physics, geology, history. Worked for ARCO as a geophysicist. Renowned author.

If it's true there's a beginning to the physical universe, as modern cosmologists now agree, then this implies a cause that transcends the universe. If the laws of physics are fine-tuned to permit life, as contemporary physicists are discovering, then perhaps there's a designer who fine-tuned them. If there's information in the cell, as molecular biology shows, then this suggests intelligent design. To get life going in the first place would have required biological information; the implications point beyond the material realm to a prior intelligent cause. (74)

You can invoke neither time nor space nor matter nor energy nor the laws of nature to explain the origin of the universe. General relativity points to the need for a cause that transcends those domains. And theism affirms the existence of such an entity— namely God. (77)

William Lane Craig, PhD, ThD, b. 1949. Doctorate in cosmology. Renowned author in the fields of cosmology, philosophy, and theology.

In response to an article about quantum theory that described subatomic particles, Dr. Craig said,

These subatomic particles ... are called "virtual particles." They are theoretical entities, and it's not even clear that they actually exist as oppose to being merely theoretical constructs. However, there's a much more important point to be made about this. You see, these particles, if they are real, do not come out of nothing. The quantum vacuum is not what most people envision when they think of a vacuum–that is absolutely nothing. On the contrary, it's a sea of fluctuating energy, an arena of violent activity that has a rich physical structure and can be described by physical laws. These particles are thought to originate by fluctuations of the energy in the "vacuum."

So it's not an example of something coming into being out of nothing, or something coming into being without a cause. The quantum vacuum and the energy locked up in the vacuum are the cause of these particles. And then we have to ask, well, what is the origin of the whole quantum vacuum itself? Where does it come from?

You've simply pushed back the issue of creation. Now you have to account for how this very active ocean of fluctuating energy came into being. Do you see what I'm saying? If quantum physical laws operate within the domain described by quantum physics, you can't legitimately use quantum physics to explain the origin of that domain itself. You need something transcendent that's beyond that domain in order to explain how the entire domain came into being. Suddenly we're back to the origins question.

Sir Fred Hoyle, 1915–2001. Eminent English astrophysicist. Cambridge. Gold Medal of the Royal Astronomical Society.

> I do not believe that any scientists who examined the evidence would fail to draw the inference that the laws of nuclear physics have been deliberately designed with regard to the consequences they produce inside stars. (127)

Paul Davies, PhD, b. 1946. Theoretical physicist, cosmologist, astrobiologist, prolific science author.

> Through my scientific work I have come to believe more and more strongly that the physical universe is put together with an ingenuity so astonishing that I cannot accept it merely as a brute fact. I cannot believe that our existence in this universe is a mere quirk of fate, an accident of history, an incidental blip in the great cosmic drama. (127)

Patrick Glynn, PhD, b. 1951. Physicist. Converted from atheism. Senior technical policy advisor for the Office of the Deputy Director for Science Programs at the US Department of Energy. Former professor at Georgetown, former arms negotiator for the Reagan Administration.

> All of the seemingly arbitrary and unrelated constants in physics have one strange thing in common—these are precisely the values you need if you want to have a universe capable of producing life. (126)

The second author is Jonathan Sarfati. Even though his PhD is in physical chemistry, he achieved honors in inorganic chemistry, condensed matter physics, and nuclear physics. He has written a book called *By Design: Evidence for Nature's Intelligent Designer—the*

God of the Bible (Creation Ministries International, 2008). In this book, he presents very detailed explanations of multiple discoveries that lead to the conclusion, if not proof, that the theory of purely physical world evolution is not only unprovable but is riddled with so many fallacies that it's not even a theory based upon proper science. Further, he states science has in fact discovered so many complex facts of physical world existence that require such a complex starting point that an intelligent Creator is the only explanation. This book is very detailed and covers innumerable scientifically proven facts, and I'm certain anyone who has a desire to learn about these things and has a scientific inclination would thoroughly enjoy every page. I picked up on a couple of summary themes that really struck me.

The first theme is irreducible complexity. Biochemist Michael Behe (b. 1952) is famous for introducing this phrase.

> Dr Sarfati: "He expounded on the discoveries of biochemical processes and sub-microscopic machinery that Darwin never dreamed of." (11)

> Dr Behe: "By irreducible complexity I mean a single system which is composed of several interacting parts that contribute to the basic function, and where the removal of any one of the parts causes the system to effectively cease functioning. An irreducibly complex system cannot be produced gradually, by slight, successive modifications of a precursor system, since any precursor to an irreducibly complex system is by definition non-functional. Since natural selection requires a function to select, an irreducibly complex biological system, if there is such a thing, would have to arise as an integrated unit for natural selection to have anything to act on. It is almost universally conceded that such a sudden event would be irreconcilable with the gradualism Darwin envisioned." (11)

Dr. Sarfati then uses several chapters to describe in fascinating detail, including quotes from multiple scientists, several existing, natural, irreducibly complex systems. He organizes them by functions like eyes and sight, hearing, smelling, navigation (e.g., dolphins), colors and patterns (e.g., certain butterflies), and flight. He concludes the flight section with a summary statement.

> The animal kingdom has used four main ways to solve the problem of heavier-than-air flight, as exemplified by birds, bats, pterosaurs and insects. All exploit the principles of aerodynamics in ingenious ways that aircraft designers are still learning. The new discoveries of the ingenuity of designs of flying creatures, as well as the continued lack of discoveries of transitional forms, remain huge obstacles to belief in evolution. (82)

There are a few quotes I picked out regarding scientific timing problems with evolution, if it's true, taking longer than life has existed, as well as scientific probability (improbability) that life evolved.

Michael Denton, PhD, born 1943, is a molecular biologist with his doctorate in biochemistry who, as of the time of this quote, is not a Creationist. He has come to the conclusion that Darwinian evolution is completely noncredible. He has authored a couple of books on this topic. His quote is as follows.

> Is it really credible that random processes could have constructed a reality, the smallest element of which—a functional protein or gene—is complex beyond our own creative capacities, a reality which is the very antithesis of chance, which excels in every sense anything produced by the intelligence of man? Alongside the level of ingenuity and complexity exhibited by the molecular machinery

of life, even our most advanced artefacts appear clumsy ... In practically every field of fundamental biological research ever-increasing levels of design and complexity are being revealed at an ever-accelerating rate. (153)

Here is Dr. Sarfati regarding enzymes:

One vital class of proteins is enzymes, which are catalysts—that is enzymes speed up chemical reactions without being consumed in the process. Without them, many reactions essential for life would be far too slow for life to exist. Enzyme expert Richard Wolfenden, of the University of North Carolina, showed in 1998 that a reaction 'absolutely essential' in creating the building blocks of DNA and RNA would take 78 million years in water, but was speeded up 10 to the 18th times by an enzyme. In 2003, Wolfenden found another enzyme that exceeded even that vast rate enhancement. A phosphatase, which catalyzes the splitting of phosphate bonds, magnified the reaction rate by a thousand times more ... 10 to the 21st times. This enzyme allows reactions vital for cell signaling and regulation to take place in a hundredth of a second. Without the enzyme, this reaction would take a trillion years—almost a hundred times even the supposed evolutionary age of the universe (about 15 billion years). Dr Wolfenden points out that natural selection could not have been operational until there was life, while as he says, life could not have functioned without these enzymes to speed up vital reactions enormously. (157–58)

Richard Wolfenden, PhD, born 1935, is a highly regarded enzyme expert with degrees from Princeton, Oxford, and Rockefeller Universities. He is a professor of chemistry, biochemistry, and biophysics at the University of North Carolina. Here is a short quote from him.

> Without catalysts, there would be no life at all, from microbes to humans. It makes you wonder how natural selection operated in such a way as to produce a protein that got off the ground as a primitive catalyst for such an extraordinary slow reaction. (158)

Sir Fred Hoyle (1915–2001), referenced above in Lee Strobel's book, abandoned his atheism when he considered the absurdly small probabilities of life without intelligent design. He was also quoted by Dr Sarfati.

> Imagine 10 to the 50th blind persons each with a scrambled Rubik cube, and try to conceive of the chances of them all simultaneously arriving at the solved form. You then have the chance of arriving by random shuffling, of just one of the many biopolymers on which life depends. The notion that not only the biopolymers, but the operating program of a living cell, could be arrived at by chance in a primordial organic soup here on the Earth is evidently nonsense of a high order. (159)

Sir Karl Popper, PhD (1902–1994), was a renowned philosopher of science and was quoted by Sarfati.

> What makes the origin of life and of genetic code a disturbing riddle is this: the genetic code is without any biological function unless it is translated; that

is, unless it leads to the synthesis of the proteins whose structure is laid down by the code. But ... the machinery by which the cell ... translates the code consists of at least fifty macromolecular components which are themselves coded in the DNA. Thus the code can not be translated except by using certain products of its translation. This constitutes a baffling circle; a really vicious circle, it seems, for any attempt to form a model or theory of the genesis of the genetic code. Thus we may be faced with the possibility that the origin of life (like the origin of physics) becomes an impenetrable barrier to science, and a residue to all attempts to reduce biology to chemistry and physics. (165)

One section of his book I found fascinating was where he shows that some atheists scientists are so determined that there is no Creator that when they realize that the physical world hasn't existed long enough for many natural complex systems to evolve, they resort to theorizing that life on earth must have been" seeded" by extraterrestrial aliens—a theory called directed panspermia. Dr. Francis Crick (1916–2004), one of the codiscoverers of the DNA double helix, became so frustrated with the growing knowledge that evolution doesn't fit the timing of life on earth that he came to adopt the directed panspermia theory and was quoted as saying,

What is so frustrating for our present purpose is that it seems almost impossible to give any numerical value to the probability of what seems a rather unlikely series of events ... An honest man, armed with all the knowledge available to us now, could only state that in some sense, the origin of life appears at the moment to be almost a miracle, so many are the conditions which would have had to have been satisfied to get it going ... Every time I

I Met God and Also Satan

write a paper on the origin of life, I determine I will never write another one, because there is too much speculation running after too few facts. (150)

Martin Line, a microbiologist, describes this dilemma about evolution taking longer than the existence of life on earth, and he concludes,

> Acceptance of such an extended period of evolution must however lead to the conclusion of an extra-terrestrial origin for life on Earth ... The concept of interstellar panspermia has been a philosophical luxury; it may soon become a necessity if constraints of evolutionary theory continue to conspire against an origin of life in our solar system. (151)

Then Dr. Sarfati summarizes the two main problems with this theory.

> 1—It merely pushes the problem back a step. Instead of choosing between creation and evolution for life on earth, we have to decide whether the hypothetical alien life was created or evolved; and 2—Many evolutionists claim creation is unscientific because it postulates a Creator who can't be tested in the lab. But exactly the same objection applies to aliens! (151)

SUMMARY

Atheism is simply the belief that there is no God, or an intelligent Creator of the physical universe. It is not the result of any kind of physical-world, scientific process.

Theism is the belief that there is a supernatural God, who is the super intelligent living Creator of the physical world.

The scientists who are atheists are continually frustrated by their inability to scientifically establish the absence of the living Creator, as well as their inability to establish the possibility of the origin of physical world life without a living Creator. Those who don't convert to theism continue to doggedly and futilely resort to other nonscientific theories for the origin of physical world life like the big bang theory or the directed panspermia theory. The big bang theory is simply agreeing with the Creationists that the physical world was created from nothing, except claiming with zero scientific evidence that there was no living Creator. Directed panspermia, again, simply represents the dogged belief that there is no Creator regardless of the evidence. In this theory, believers shift the debate to another physical world, saying that because our science doesn't allow evolution, there must be another physical world out there somewhere where life is, and those aliens brought it to Earth.

The scientists who are theists, on the other hand, study the same physical world phenomena and simply work in awe of the intelligence, power, and ability of the living Creator.

=9=

THE GREATEST ECLIPSE

Put on the whole armor of God, that you may be able to stand against the wiles of the devil. For we do not wrestle against flesh and blood, but against principalities, against powers, against the rulers of the darkness of this world, against spiritual wickedness in high places.

—Ephesians 6:11–12 (KJV)

Dr. Kyle said, "You were saying the 'dark force' approached your friend. Please be more specific."

"The force wasn't actually dark versus light as in colors. It was ominous and extremely powerful, and it emanated the opposite of good. The simple human description is a 'dark force.' It was simply evil and overwhelmed me as only a blast furnace of terror could. I had the terrifying, very clear awareness that it was pure evil, very alive, and seething with a malevolent intention and purpose. There was no doubt that it was focused upon my friend and me."

"I thought you had said it was headed for your friend?"

"I did. That's because it did seem to me initially focused on just my friend. However, there was no doubt that as I approached my friend, I was immediately included as part of its quarry."

"What exactly did it look like?" Dr. Kyle asked.

"It was strictly a spiritual—excuse me, non-physical-world being. It had no specific edges but a very definite, and very alive, stormy core of darkness.

"Did you have any sense of relative strength between you and it?"

"Absolutely. I immediately knew it had significantly more strength than me or my friend, and even us together. I also immediately understood that it was intent on taking possession of my friend before he figured out where he was and what was happening."

"How did you know that?"

"If you were in the wilderness somewhere, and a grizzly bear suddenly appeared and came charging at you, would you immediately conclude its intentions, or would you spend critical time analyzing its intentions? I understood its intentions more quickly and clearly than I would upon seeing any physical creature charging at my friend and me."

"Did it have a face?"

I said, "No. Neither were there any other distinguishable features other than its profound darkness and the emanating intention to consume with terrifying harm."

"Sounds like time to get out of there."

"You haven't asked how this situation made me feel. Please, for full clarity of the situation, let me share that aspect."

"Okay, what were you feeling? I assume some fear."

"I can assure you that the phrase 'some fear' is an understatement of gargantuan proportions. When watching a movie wherein a super strong, malevolent force of evil is attacking the underdog, that is frightening, and most people have experienced that kind of movie scene. While watching the most terrifying scenes, we are gripped with emotions beyond description, including physical manifestations of fear, like the chills. However, when fear from movie scenes overwhelms us, we can grab our chair, walk away, or turn off the movie. When I suddenly realized that we were facing not a movie manufactured evil but true evil, more powerful than anything that can be described physically—and that it was coming after us—the word *terrifying* doesn't describe it. I was consumed with fear and trepidation and had nowhere to hide as it approached."

"Like I said, sounds like time to get out of there."

I didn't quite know what to think about Dr. Kyle's effort to go along with my description of what happened, but it was better than the constant disbelief I had encountered from others when sharing this experience. I figured he was going to let me finish before trying to tear it apart.

On a personal note, I would love to believe that the reaction I had back then, which I was about to explain to Dr. Kyle, meant that my parents had taught me well. My parents believed that if ever faced with a situation where an enemy more powerful than us was attacking or pursuing us, and especially where *us* includes others seemingly weaker in some way that that enemy, we should fight back even it meant risking our own lives to save or assist others. I obviously survived this attack in the spiritual dimension and felt good about how I handled it, but it was actually God who had determined the outcome of the attack. Therefore, I was left to hope that I would be able to react that same way if faced with an attack by the powerful against an underdog here in a strictly physical world setting.

I responded, "I actually had the instinctive fight reaction, rather than flight. I was overcome with the awareness that I could not attempt to leave my friend alone to face this fiercely strong and nasty being empowered with evil. I knew that if I did succeed in escaping, I would never be able to live with myself for abandoning him."

"Come on, Glenn. 'Evil'?"

"Doctor, all I can tell you is that I had the experience, and there was no doubt that this monster being was evil. You can take any definition of evil ever used, and this was all of them rolled into one. I was there, I saw it, and I could feel the powerful corruption of the energy waves swarming over me as it approached."

"Okay, I'll accept that. Do you believe this was the source of evil, like Satan?"

"Since you asked, yes, I believe it was Satan, the prime angel of evil."

Dr. Kyle held up his hand. "I just got a case of the chills. I thought that the God believers claim that Satan comes in more friendly forms than this. Otherwise, how could people ever voluntarily choose him to follow instead of God?"

"Satan is a superhuman being capable of interacting himself, or sending his demons to interact, with humans in any form he chooses."

"Wow, Glenn. Don't you think we're getting a little too far away from the story of your experience?"

"I don't. It happened exactly the way I have shared it with you, and I've simply answered your questions about the dark being. Trust me, this is not the kind of experience where one forgets the details," I said with a slight smile.

"Okay. Just because I admitted getting the chills, you'd better not be flavoring it up."

"Doctor, I get the chills every moment I spend recollecting the experience, let alone telling the story. The main reason I'm talking to you about this is what happened at the end." I continued. "As I probably very stupidly approached the inevitable direct struggle with the far stronger evil force, I had no confidence of winning the battle. I simply knew that this thing was Satan himself, and I sensed that I could not give in or run in fear. I somehow believed that fighting with my last shred of existence was my only choice.

"Then I began to sense that I was part of an eclipse. It was as though I was blocking the sun from shining on the earth. From behind me, I sensed a bright light full of force approaching. The next few events all happened within mere moments in our sense of time, definitely within less time than it will take to describe what happened."

"Especially if you don't get on with it."

"Okay, as I attempted to turn toward this newly arriving Bright Force, I couldn't look directly at Its blinding brightness. It was simply brightness beyond description! Even cleaner and more pure than sunlight, if that makes sense. It emanated an energy that was overwhelmingly powerful yet comforting beyond description. Its presence brought a kind of warming wind that I could sense was more powerful than the cold and malevolent energy emanating from the dark force.

"I was virtually caught in a storm of competing powerful winds blowing in opposite directions. My concern and fear were calmed as I sensed that the warming winds from the Bright Force were easily stronger than those form the dark force.

"Then as the Bright Force was zooming in to the battleground proximity, It spoke to me in a very clear voice."

Dr. Kyle started to say something, but then he waved for me to continue. His eyes indicated he was very involved in the story whether he liked it or not, and he was anxious to hear what the bright force had to say.

"The Bright Force said, 'Get back to your body where you belong, for now.'

"I started to say, 'But my friend.'

"Before I could get that complete thought out, the Bright Force continued.

'I'll take care of this.' Then it was as though It extended a part of Itself as a wind. I was caught up and blown toward an interdimensional course, back toward my body in the physical world.

"I was literally on the way back, when the most shrilling, blood-curdling sounds ever heard filled the atmosphere of that dimension. The worst screams and screeches ever produced in the scariest movies don't come close. I understood that these were the anguished screams of Satan as it fought for and lost control of the souls that had inadvertently found their way out of the physical world without experiencing physical death.

"My last two thoughts as I exited that dimension were a question and its immediate answer. Why would Satan be so anguished over losing these two particular souls this way? Then an answer occurred to me. Imagine the value to Satan of being able to take control of two souls and then send them back to their living physical bodies as his emissaries? Now it's okay to get the chills. But it isn't over yet."

Dr. Kyle said, "I thought you described the last events prior to exiting this expanded reality dimension."

"I did. However, I then found myself back in my physical body, sitting in the dorm room. I was both chilled and thrilled to the bone. I then noticed my friend's seemingly lifeless body sitting in his corner of the room. It seemed that he had not returned. Then he commenced rhythmically repeating the command or plea: 'No, no, no ...' I went to him and tried to talk to him, but I was overcome with terror when I realized he seemed trapped between the two dimensions. Then suddenly he jumped up and hollered, 'Never do that to me again!'

"I said, 'It's okay, we're back.' I asked him if he was talking to me about never doing that again, because I hadn't done anything to him. When I tried to talk about the fantastically extraordinary experience we had just completed, his eyes glazed over for a minute. Then he said he didn't know what I was talking about. He never did acknowledge the experience for whatever reason, which obviously left me alone to deal with it."

=10=

TICKET TO PERMANENT PARADISE

Now this I say brethren, that flesh and blood cannot inherit the kingdom of God; nor does corruption inherit incorruption.... For the trumpet will sound, and the dead will be raised incorruptible, and *we* shall be changed. For this corruption must put on incorruption, and this mortal *must* put on immortality.

—1 Corinthians 15:50, 52–53 (NKJV)

"So you're telling me that you met God and Satan?"

"Yes."

"No wonder those others you tried to talk to long ago threw you out."

"Usually, I didn't get to that part of the experience before they quit listening. In one case, the listener allowed me to get into this part of the experience and then held up their fingers to me in the form of a cross and asked me to stop."

"That was true of God-fearing religious people?"

"Yes. It seemed that the people I was talking to then wanted to believe they understood the complete breadth of God's interaction with humans. One Bible scholar even stated that the only humans God directly interacted with were the biblically famous ones whose stories were in the Bible to give us guidance, adding that God doesn't do that anymore because we have all the guidance God intended, written in the Bible."

"Regardless of their reasons, you must understand how ridiculous this account sounds to the rational mind."

I knew what I was inclined to say at this point, but how could it be addressed without insulting the esteemed Dr. Kyle? After sitting quietly for a short while and contemplating this critical moment in our dialogue, I gave it a whirl.

"Dr. Kyle, my gut reaction is to simply observe that I consider myself rational, and I experienced it." I paused briefly for emphasis. "I have more to say, and I have no desire for this to sound insulting to you or any of the doubting, rational people."

"Sounds like you are about to insult me," he said with a wry smile. To me, the smile was the green light to proceed.

"Everyone who has reacted to my story of this experience with fear or skepticism has had that reaction strictly based upon their preconceived notion of reality."

Dr. Kyle responded, "Now I believe I see what all that discussion about the boundaries of reality was about. Is that right?"

"Exactly. I have come to understand that most people tend to have a concept for the boundaries of reality that they will allow to be utilized in their thinking. And that is true whether or not they are believers in the existence of the supernatural God. The atheists eliminate God from consideration in their observances of the reality around them. Many believers simply add the existence of a distant God-being to that same set of observances of reality. It seems that most believers simply don't give much thought to the actual dimensions of reality. Once they accept through reasonableness that there is a powerful God out there somewhere, it is easy to accept the existence of a heaven 'up there somewhere' and a 'hell down there somewhere.'"

"Are you saying the believers are not actually true believers unless they accept what you experienced?"

"Not at all. I'm just observing how they can justify discounting my story. From what I have read and understand about God's word in the Bible, God discloses that there are mysteries of reality normally held back from disclosure to the human mind. Further, regardless of what level of mysteries have been disclosed to any one person while residing in a human body, there is only one thing that determines that person's ultimate destiny. This 'ticket to eternal paradise' is obtained by simply choosing to believe in God and His resurrection of Jesus, and inviting Them to send the Holy Spirit to live inside you. This is a simple act based upon a simple decision and results in punching one's ticket to eternal paradise, regardless of what mysteries of reality one has come to understand, how intelligent one is, or how hard one works at doing good deeds."

There was a long pause while I contemplated how the conversation had gone directly to the "ticket to paradise" concept. I had not planned to say those things at this point. They simply came out as the flow of the discussion progressed. He was probably wondering the same thing.

"Glenn, how did we get from your encounter with God and its implications to somehow discussing Jesus and the Bible? I am aware that the Old Testament is mainly about God's relationship with man, if it's all true. However, you have jumped to including Jesus in our discussion, and therefore your reference to the Bible includes the New Testament as well. I am not aware that we have connected your experience to the New Testament of the Bible or Jesus."

Here we go again, I thought. It looks like I did jump right over a key conclusion I came to in my life. In my mind, I saw Dr. Kyle as the logic vulture: he devoured illogical the same as a vulture devours the lifeless.

At least I had an answer that gives life to the connection I had passed over. We would see if he agreed. Obviously, if he didn't, he'd attack, shred it apart, and consume it as a celebratory meal in honor of logic conquering the illogical. I gave it a shot.

"Sorry, Doctor. I guess I jumped ahead a little there. As you evidently know, there are sixty-six books in the combined Old and New Testament Christian Bible. They contain historical accounts, powerful quotes, and a lot of lessons to be learned about humans' life on this earth."

"Glenn," Dr. Kyle interrupted, "I didn't ask you about an overview of the Bible components. I asked how you personally came to bring Jesus into your story."

I was inclined to respond, "Yes, sir, Mr. Vulture," but I kept my cool and continued.

"I referenced the volume of the Bible to start my answer, in order to be able to emphasize how simple it is to get the main parts and the Jesus connection."

He responded without hesitation. "Why waste time talking about extraneous things to your answer, if your answer is so simple?"

This time I didn't acquiesce to his tempo and direction. "Dr. Kyle, I referenced the entire Judeo-Christian Bible because once the most powerful and yet simple points are extracted from it, the rest becomes a valuable, complementary source of intellectual and spiritual nourishment to guide humans while they reside in their earthly bodies."

Now for the simple. "The knowledge that God exists is a motivator for reading the Old Testament, which is where the relationship between God and earthly man commenced. Within those writings are prophecies, hundreds of which have already come true in human earthly history. I find it extremely interesting that one of those prophecies, which was foretold in multiple Old Testament instances, was the birth of Jesus, and that it was to take place in Bethlehem. This was prophesied hundreds of years before it happened. To me, that is the most powerful fact, among others, that is so simple, and it definitely connects the two testaments of the Judeo-Christian Bible."

"It sounds like you have accepted the New Testament as a critical source of information with only one reason."

"Not at all, Doctor. There is also the volume of accounts of eyewitnesses that saw and communicated with Jesus after his crucifixion. There were over five hundred people who saw him with his resurrected body."

He interrupted me. "That's your total reasoning?"

"I wasn't done yet. I have a couple more reasons. First, there is a rarely discussed fact presented by the apostle John in the book of John: chapter 12, verse 42. As you probably know, it is generally thought, or at least easily accepted, that the religious leaders in that area during that era—"

"You mean the Jewish leaders, right?" he interrupted.

"Exactly—Jewish religious leaders. As I was saying, although it was the Jewish leaders in control that forced the crucifixion of Jesus by the Romans, there were actually multiple leaders who came to believe in Jesus as the Son of God. According to John in the verse I referenced, 'Nevertheless, even among the [local Jewish] rulers, many believed in Him, but because of the Pharisees they did not confess Him, lest they should be put out of the synagogue.'

"You're right that I've never heard of that verse. Was that your two additional reasons?"

"No. Second, there's also the fact that against all rational thinking and odds, a large number of those eyewitnesses I referred to prior to John's quote completely changed their lives and gave the balance of their earthly existence to teaching what Jesus taught. Furthermore, one of the greatest skeptics of those days, a highly educated Old Testament scholar, and the most famous persecutor of Christians claimed to have met the resurrected Jesus and then became one of the greatest teachers of the Gospel."

"You're talking about Paul?"

"Yes. Originally Saul of Tarsus, renamed Paul after his meeting with Jesus. As I'm sure you know, he actually wrote letters that make up a large portion of the New Testament after his conversion, and during a time when he gave 100 percent of the rest of his life to Jesus's teachings."

"I'm listening."

"Okay. Then once you start reading about Jesus, his teachings, and the books written by his followers in the New Testament, the ultimate ticket to permanent paradise becomes obvious and boils down to something very simple. This simple truth is referenced a few different places, but my favorite is in the book of John, chapter 3, verses 1 to 21, where Jesus's discussion with the Pharisee Nicodemus succinctly outlines the most powerful conclusions about humans obtaining their ticket to paradise following Jesus's time on earth. Once a human chooses to believe the truth of Jesus being the Son of God and chooses to be born again spiritually, he or she has received the ticket to permanent paradise. Some other quotes from Jesus explain that being spiritually born again includes inviting and accepting the Holy Spirit into your spirit or heart. That's pretty simple."

"What about Jesus dying for the sins of humans, like we are always hearing from Christians?"

"Well, that's automatically included in what I described. Believing Jesus is the Son of God requires believing the entire New Testament story as told over and over again in many parts and in many ways throughout its books and chapters. Actually, this specific point is once again very simple logically. It says in the New Testament that Jesus died as a payment for human sin, just like prior to Jesus's presence on Earth, humans had to make sacrifices for their sins. Now that your sins have been paid for, the only requirement God left for you to get your permanent ticket to paradise is to believe the truth that your sins have been paid for by Jesus ('the key part of the whole truth of Jesus being the Son of God') and to accept the Holy Spirit from God as a companion and helper in your life ('being born again')."

"Are you saying this ticket is permanent, or that the paradise you have the ticket to is permanent?"

"I agree that is a great question, Doctor, and I think I can apply some simple logic toward the answer."

I wanted to jump up and cheer for myself. I thought that I, instead of him, came up with the logic thing twice in a row.

"Logic sounds good," he retorted. "Let's hear it."

"Okay. If you destroy a ticket for a plane trip, you can no longer board the plane."

"That's obvious. I'm waiting to see the logical connection to eternal paradise."

Obviously, logic and patience were not related to each other. He had no patience but doggedly demanded logic. "I'm getting there," I replied. "I understand that there are many followers of Jesus who have disagreements about this, and though I am not a Bible scholar, it seems to me that this is as simple as examining what actually makes up the ticket. If you haven't changed what made up the ticket, you haven't changed the ticket. Therefore, as long as you don't somehow purposefully choose to reject the truth of Jesus and His sacrifice, and kick God's Spirit companion out of your life, you still have the ticket."

"Wow, Glenn. Logically, you are saying that Christians can commit bad behaviors and retain the ticket to eternal paradise."

"I agree. After all, because there is no permanent perfection within the physical universe, then logic dictates that there are no perfect humans. I realize that many, including myself, have struggled with this concept because we want for there to be perfection somewhere, and especially within a life turned over to God's direction and influence. This is where reading the volumes of stories and narratives within the Bible provides assistance. The Bible is filled with stories about people who did great things for God and who, in their day-to-day lives, committed behaviors and actions less than— and in some cases, far from—perfectly.

"Also included within the Bible are descriptions of crowns received in paradise regarding one's actions and behaviors while still in their physical bodies. This fact implies that there are different possible posts or assignments in paradise. It's in the Bible, and taken together with Jesus's teachings that we are not to seek justice, the logical conclusion that one's ticket is not lost due to any certain bad behavior seems to be solidly affirmed. It is also true that there are many teachings in the Bible about how to improve one's quality of life by attempting to get as close to God as possible, which logically includes working on improving one's behaviors and actions.

"There is also teaching about not judging others. This again follows the logic of the components of the ticket to paradise. It is clearly outlined within the scriptures that even if one is among the best at maintaining 'good' behaviors, judging others' behaviors is itself a bad thing.

"There is also forgiveness. What is explained about God's forgiveness in the Bible also complements the truth regarding the ticket to paradise being so simple. When one obtains the ticket, one desires to behave better. One also learns about the power of forgiveness and that to trigger that power, there has to be repentance for bad behaviors. The important thing here is that a bad behavior doesn't cancel the prized ticket; it simply commences a series of interactions with God and Jesus that are designed to accomplish a perfect forgiveness for the bad behavior. By perfect forgiveness, I mean acknowledging the sin to God and expressing appreciation to Jesus and Him for having paid the price for it and forgiven it."

Dr. Kyle sat there through this entire description, which was my best effort to logically answer questions about the concept of the simplicity of the punched ticket to paradise. I wondered where we had gone to regarding his acceptance of my OBE and the whole God and Jesus discussion.

He changed the subject a little. "I find your discussion of God, heaven, and hell interesting. You gave me the feeling that in addition to encountering God, you think there are more places or dimensions to reality than the average religious person believes. I want to come back to Descartes, but first tell me how your experience impacted your understanding of the dimensions of reality."

Wow. Instead of total rejection, Dr. Kyle had engaged in a discussion of the meanings of my experience. I wondered whether he has accepted that God existed, or he was just trying to set me up for a logic power punch that he may be readying for his attempted knock-out blow to my story.

"Well, first of all, my conclusions regarding Descartes's statement and the dimensions of reality can be discussed together in wrapping all of this up. Earlier, I said that Descartes was wrong because we obviously exist aside from having thoughts about physical world things. It's obviously possible that Descartes was contemplating a larger reality and that we exist independent of our physical bodies. Even in that context, I submit that my experience proves the existence of an all-powerful Creator who created us and the entire physical universe, and who maintains control over the entire physical world dimension. Therefore, we are God's creation, come into existence at his will, are put into physical bodies, and then learn thinking skills. So Descartes was simply wrong—we are, and then we think.

"Okay, so your whole Descartes thing was just a ruse to get to this discussion?"

"No, not at all. The Descartes experiment was logically pursued, and the results ended up being more profound than just the answer to the original question.

"This sounds a lot like the discussion we had about the scientific process, with logic tests and experiments leading to conclusions beyond the original pursuit."

"Yes, it does."

After a long, contemplative silence, the professor asked, "After your experience, what do you think about the heaven and hell dimensions that are so popular with religious people?"

"Dr. Kyle, this is a great question. Based upon my experience, I find it very simple and logical to accept the existence of these places."

"You mean because you know that God exists, you can accept these religiously defined places?"

"No. First, based upon my experience, I know firsthand two major facts: one, that God, the all-powerful Creator, exists, and two, that there are dimensions of reality beyond and separate from the physical universe. Second, with this factual knowledge, many biblical teachings and the stories in them that previously seemed mystical are now far more understandable with my simple mind."

"Okay, like I asked, what is your take on heaven and hell? Which place were you in when you had this experience?"

"First of all, one of the biggest insights gained from the experience is that when attempting to contemplate and understand how physical and spiritual realities fit together, perspective is everything. The perspective that we are at the center of things in our physical world human existence clearly limits our ability to perceive anything beyond the physical world. When, or if, we encounter evidence of a larger reality, we tend to distort and inappropriately rearrange our thinking so we can fit what we encountered into our preconceived, physical-world-oriented, and unfortunately very limited perspective of the dimensions of reality.

"An example of this perspective issue is to compare viewing the physical world by standing outside a building and looking around, or going to outer space and looking back at the Earth. The simple roundness of the Earth is difficult, if not impossible, to decipher by standing on the ground and looking down the street, but it's obvious from space."

"That's a simple enough concept. How are you trying to relate it to the biblical heaven and hell?"

"What I'm trying to say is that attempting to understand these things while remaining grounded in a physical-world perspective is like standing outside your house and trying to completely understand that the earth is round. Removing your perspective to a spiritual, non-physical-world perspective and seeing the physical world as a small subset of reality is like looking at the Earth from space to understand more easily about the Earth."

Dr. Kyle said, "Interesting. Now can you try to answer my question, please?"

"Sorry if that seemed too simple, but it's very powerful. Once you can place your perspective for observations out into the expanded, non-physical-world dimension of existence, and you look back and see the entire physical universe as a created subset of all reality, then the logic and possibility of the existence of other subsets or dimensions of reality is extremely easy to accept and understand."

"So you are saying that heaven and hell are two dimensions of reality beyond the physical universe? If so, let's get back to my question. Which one were you in?"

"To your first question, yes, heaven and hell are two dimensions of non-physical-world reality. To your second question, I was in neither."

"Just when I thought we were getting somewhere with the consistency of your story."

"Wait a minute. There has been nothing inconsistent. Remember, I have not claimed that God took me on a tour of all dimensions of reality unlocking all mysteries for me. I just know that he saved me from a potential bad outcome of my inadvertent trip to a dimension of the nonphysical world, and then he sent me back to finish living this life inside this physical human body. My experience was not generated from reading the Bible, however regarding your question about heaven and hell, let's allow that they are biblically described places.

"On a very basic level, heaven is described as a place God has as His protected home domain, and in which He has reserved spots for good beings and souls that have lived in an earthly body and made the decision to believe in God and his resurrection of Jesus, once their physical body dies. According to the Bible, Satan was cast out of heaven. Satan came to my friend and me, and therefore we were not in heaven."

"Likewise, hell is described with several different, very nasty descriptions as a place of evil and misery. It's the bottomless pit where God cast Satan in the Bible prophecies. I do not believe we were in that place because we could move about freely while feeling exhilarated and having only good feelings. Further, we were not people who had rejected God.

"The bottom line is that my experience and logic established that there are a minimum of four different dimensions of living reality: a minimum of three separate dimensions, which are subsets of a master dimension, and the fourth is a master dimension. We all have some level of familiarity with the three separate subset dimensions of reality, which are generally described as the physical world, heaven, and hell. There is at least one additional dimension, which I call the master dimension, because it is a general dimension that contains, or surrounds, those three."

"I'm glad you said *logic*. Please explain. Your experience has identified only two places, as best as I can track your story: the physical world, and where you were."

"Okay. I experienced a God who was all-powerful and in charge of everything comprehendible. Logic led me to read the Bible for explanations and guidance for things encountered regarding God. I would be happy to examine another source for issues regarding God if they're as credible and consistent a source as the Judeo-Christian Bible."

"Your logic is okay. I may want to examine the Bible with you later regarding using it as a resource. I noticed you used the word *minimum* for the number of dimensions. Why?"

"Well, I have explained how I got up to four dimensions. That was through my experience and then reading the Bible for logical clarifications. The simple fact that I realize how limited the human perspective is compared to God's means I am in no position to believe I can know all that God knows. Therefore, God may have other dimensions for purposes beyond my comprehension and beyond my need-to-know clearance."

Then Dr. Kyle threw a curveball. "What about all of the extraterrestrials that have supposedly been documented as visiting Earth?"

Now I knew I had to be careful. First of all, I figured that he must not actually believe in extraterrestrials due to his generally earthbound parameters for accepting things as facts. But then again, maybe he had an experience in this regard that had been part of his cause for not accepting God. I had given this some thought, but I didn't want to walk into one of his traps and lose him.

I took my shot and tried to throw out a little humor. "Are you inquiring whether my experience was actually some sort of transportation to an interstellar location, by some extraterrestrial but physical beings?" I smiled and waited.

He stared at me for a minute and then finally smiled. "I'm just curious what you think about this subject matter."

"Dr. Kyle, you've surprised me with this question. I'm not sure what causes you to ask this, but I do know that there are many stories and documentaries out there that seem to document some unknown beings with superhuman powers or equipment that seem supernatural."

He interrupted me with a grin. "Yeah, and how does all of that fit your description of expanded reality?"

He still was avoiding the delivery of a clue as to what he may or may not already believe, so I plodded ahead. I felt I had no choice because I couldn't guess what was on his mind regarding spacemen and UFOs.

"I actually believe, and I think logically, that it doesn't really matter, considering what we know is important for our permanent existence. I think that there are several possibilities regarding how extraterrestrials fit into the basic minimum of four dimensions. Here are the possibilities the way I see it."

1. They actually do not exist as non-human beings. Possibly all of the sightings and encounters reported are either not real, or they're based upon actual top-secret operations of existing earthly governments.

2. They could be angels from the dimension of God's domain interacting with earth for some good, God-sponsored purpose.

3. They could be minions of Satan sent by the sponsor of evil to interact with earth for purposes we would consider very derogatory and counter to God's plan for us on Earth.

4. They could be from yet another dimension beyond the four I have described.

"Why don't you think these possibilities are important?" he queried.

"Because the four dimensions I have described include all aspects of how we, who have souls sent to be in an earthly body in this physical world dimension, get from these earthly decaying bodies to an eternal paradise. That story is complete regardless of which of these four possibilities regarding extraterrestrials are true."

"Wow, Glenn," he responded. "It sounds like you've given this some thought." He paused. And here it came. "But it seems you've dismissed this whole concept a little too easily." He was maintaining his cool demeanor without expression. I hadn't picked up even a hint as to why he had brought this topic up.

"Have you had some sort of encounter yourself, Doctor?"

With a short laugh, he leaned back in his chair. "No, Glenn. I was just curious and wondered whether you had thought much about this issue."

"Okay, well, I don't think I have dismissed the issue too easily. In fact, I have not literally dismissed it at all. I have used only logic to figure out that it doesn't really matter regarding my ticket to permanent paradise."

I was pretty impressed with how I emphasized the use of logic, but he wasn't.

"I don't think your four possibilities included the actual possibility that these potential beings are in fact from another celestial body within the physical universe."

"You're right, I didn't mention that. But from what I've read, the odds of another planet being able to support humanoid life are extremely small to nonexistent. So probably that belief of mine caused me to slip up and leave that out. Logically, it would seem that possibility is actually part of my number four."

"So you're saying that another planet and another non-physical-world dimension are the same thing?"

Whoops. I had gotten too relaxed and comfortable in the conversation, and he caught this point like he snagged every piece of illogical or ill-fitting information and destroyed it out of a compulsion for perfection. I attempted to clarify.

"No, they're not the same thing. I meant they have the same consequence to what matters. Technically, I should have listed number five as 'another physical world planet.' But that doesn't make the consequence of that potential truth any more relevant to humans getting to permanent paradise than if they are from another dimension interacting with our physical world dimension. And my out-of-body experience certainly had nothing to do with this topic." There he sat in deep thought, staring through me. I waited. He finally responded. "I understand, and I have another question for you. In my reading about the various OBEs and NDEs, I noticed that it seemed common for the NDE people to have felt they were in a tunnel heading toward a light. Do you have any thoughts about that description?"

"Actually, I do. And it is an integral part of the multiple dimension conclusion."

"What in the world do you mean by that?"

"This is just my theory, but it seems logical to me. You see, my experience caused me to wonder about people's souls getting from their body to paradise when their bodies die. I realize this is not a common question among believers because it is generally accepted by them that souls simply leave the body and go to 'heaven' if that is their destiny. However, I learned for a fact that it is possible to leave the body and not necessarily go immediately to paradise or a bad place, but rather exist in a nonphysical spiritual zone. Further, I learned that the bad force, as well as God himself, can exist and travel within that zone or dimension.

"Therefore, the famous 'tunnel' could be God's mechanism to safely transport souls through that generally accessible dimension directly to His protected paradise or heaven."

"Do you think that Satan believes in God?"

"Wow, that's an interesting question. I also happen to think it's an extremely important one, and I'm glad you asked. It seems obvious that Satan believes the all-powerful God does exist. In my personal experience, God whipped up on Satan, which certainly indicates Satan believes there is a God. The conventional biblical teaching is that Satan is an angel who rebelled against God, and ever since that occurrence, it follows up by spending energy attempting to influence souls still residing in their temporary physical-world bodies to reject God and Christ."

"Well, where does Satan primarily reside in the four-dimensional reality you have described?"

The professor just gave an opening to discuss the most important thing of all, regardless of how many dimensions there are.

"Dr. Kyle, as I have mentioned, I met Satan in the dimension that I have labeled as the master dimension. Everything else I have to say about this is based upon reading and, I hope, a little logic. I realize the simplified view is that nonbelievers reside in hell, and that includes Satan. However, Satan obviously believes that God is real and that the New Testament story of Jesus is true. That's why he showed up in the early days of Jesus's teachings to tempt Jesus and try to get him to not follow through with his mission on Earth. Therefore, it seems logical that Satan spends time in the bad eternal places, whether we call them hell, bottomless pit, or whatever. He obviously also spends time in the master dimension, and at the very least, he has direct interaction with the physical world, where his self-imposed mission is to get souls residing within their temporary human bodies to reject God's plan for their permanent, ultimate existence in the good place."

"So you are saying that people who believe that God is real can still go to a bad place for their permanent existence after leaving their temporary physical bodies?"

The professor was discussing this like he was sitting in a Bible study group. I couldn't tell if he had chosen to believe in God during our interactions, or whether he was trying to set me up as the next target in his shooting range. In any event, he'd opened a discussion where the most important thing about our existence was the answer to his question. We'd see how this went.

"As you know, there are many people who, once they have accepted the reality of the existence of God, think that simply believing that God is real is their ticket to eternal paradise. However, Satan believes that God exists, and he has been thrown out of God's eternal paradise based upon his rebellion against God's plan for harmonious existence. Therefore, using simple logic, there has to be something more to obtaining that prized ticket to God's heaven than just believing that Gods exists. Relying upon the writings I am aware of in the Bible, the true ticket to paradise comes from not only accepting the truth of God's existence but also the truth of Jesus's teachings that He was sent to the physical world to become the sacrifice for all of our bad stuff, and that we must invite God to send to us a spirit to live in and with us and help us get through the remainder of our existence in our temporary physical bodies."

Dr. Kyle sat there staring at me for a while, and then he finally spoke.

"You seem to have gone from logical discussion to street corner preaching. I have to go right now. Let's try to wrap this up next Tuesday." Then he got up and walked out.

Wow, here we went again. We'd already covered the wild experience. Was he actually losing interest in the ramifications of the meeting with God?

=11=

GOOD AND BAD THINGS, GOOD AND BAD PEOPLE

And as we have borne the image of the man of dust,
we shall also bear the image of the heavenly *Man*.
—1 Corinthians 15:49 (NKJV)

Well, at least Dr. Kyle showed up smiling and emanating a friendly demeanor.

"Glenn, we ended up last time with you saying that you believe there is more to getting to the permanent paradise dimension that just believing that God exists. Although I'm fascinated by the dimensions explanation—and just so you know, I'm accepting, at least in theory, the possibility of its existence—I believe that the rational conclusion of how it fits with your other ideas about Christianity are critical in order for me to arrive at a full acceptance of the theory. I would like to hear more about how you think it all fits together."

"Dr. Kyle, I have concluded that even with my traveling to other dimensions, the ultimate truth of our existence is very simple and straightforward regardless of how many dimensions there are. I met God, so I know He exists. I have read about His plan regarding the physical world. It all boils down to the simple truth that can be shared by a big-time, polished television preacher or a street corner preacher: that getting right with God while still in our physical bodies is the key to ultimate understanding and permanently dwelling with God in His paradise. If we don't make that decision, then we are destined for bad stuff because we have rejected God's plan, and we aren't going to care about how many dimensions there are while we are stuck in a miserable dimension. An interesting story told by Jesus in Luke 16:19–31 made an impact upon me regarding dimensions."

"Wait a minute. You have the verse citation memorized?"

"Well, I recalled the story, and since our last meeting, I refreshed my mind by looking it up again. Can I relay the passage?"

"Sure, go ahead."

"It was about a rich man and a beggar named Lazarus. Jesus described the horrible condition of Lazarus, including that dogs were licking his sores. But more important, he was situated outside the rich man's gate, and his greatest hope was for crumbs from the rich man's home. Then they both died. Lazarus found himself with Abraham in heaven, and the rich man found himself in hades, tormented including with flame. The rich man begged Abraham for some water to cool his torment. Abraham responded that there is a great divide, and those who are in heaven cannot pass to there. Neither can those where he is pass to heaven."

"Glenn, I think I heard that story when I was a kid. I think I see why it interested you regarding this dimensions theory."

"Of course. In this story, Jesus himself is explaining that there are two dimensions separated from each other, and the people whose physical bodies have died have been assigned to one or the other and cannot traverse back and forth. Of important note, these are also dimensions where people go after their human bodies have died, so these are not part of the physical world dimension in which we currently live. Thus, the three subdimensions—the temporary physical world, and the two permanent destinations for the souls of the humans whose bodies die."

"And in review, you are saying your OBE took you to a master dimension?"

"Exactly. The physical world is obviously limited to physical things, and the master dimension allows travel between dimensions, whereas the more permanent destinations for the souls initially assigned to human bodies do not."

"Okay, let's say all of that is true. What do you think about the story of Jesus, in a physical body, ascending to heaven in view of his disciples? That would seem to conflict with the other dimensions not being physical."

"Actually, because you are familiar with that story, you may be familiar with other teachings in the Bible about souls currently existing within their physical world bodies being given new bodies when they are accepted to God's eternal paradise. Clearly it is logical that with the knowledge that God exists, the stories of Jesus's ascension, and the descriptions of souls receiving new bodies for their existence in heaven, are perfectly consistent. It seems logically obvious that although the bodies that souls receive for existence in heaven may be very similar to our earthly bodies in appearance, they will be permanent and nondecaying in nature."

"So do you think the souls that end up in the bad permanent place have bodies other than the vaguely describable spiritual form you experienced?"

"Neither my experience nor any time I've spent reading and thinking about this have lead me to any belief or theory about that, logical or otherwise. My experience confirms, without having to choose to believe it, that God does exist. It also leads to the rational and logical conclusion about the dimensions of reality. The dimensions explanation is simply an unveiling of things that were previously mysterious to many of us and, it seems to me, makes it easier to believe the basics about God and His plan as explained in the Bible.

"The multiple dimensions of reality concept has the potential to provide many very simple answers to many questions that linger in the minds of both God believers and nonbelievers. A simple yet powerful example is heaven. It is a place described in the Bible, yet no one, believer nor nonbeliever, can find it with a telescope. Believers are left to believe that it is a true place, but its precise location is a mystery. Even believers have trouble with this because its physical location can't be found with the most powerful instrument designed to enhance physical eyesight. The implication they are left with is that it is very distant, yet some of them have interactions that indicate it didn't take much for a resident of heaven, like an angel, to appear before them, or for Jesus to get there when the disciples saw him ascending to it and disappearing before their eyes. Once it is accepted that everything that exists is not necessarily made up of physical-world particles, but that there are nonphysical places with very live beings, like the non-physical-world dimensions that I have described, then the idea of the heaven described in the Bible is much easier to accept. Instead of being located in a physically distant place that remains a mystery, it is actually, in a physical sense, right next door. A person simply passes from the physical dimension to the heaven dimension if that is his or her permanent destiny."

It was as though the professor's eyes were an x-ray machine. He seemed to look right through me. His thoughts seemed to have caught a ride on some sort of mystical wave passing through the room. Finally, he focused on me and spoke.

"Well, at least I can say that you seemed to have given this some thought as well. I was just reflecting on various concepts or mysteries to which your theory may be relevant. One thing that I was always skeptical about regarding God and the Bible is the various descriptions of different bodies. This fascinating theory is not so bad based upon what you experienced, Glenn. Assuming all of this is true, you must have come to conclusions about why some humans who've accepted Christ don't seem to reflect perfectly good behaviors. Any ideas there?"

The professor surely understood that my brief yet powerful experience didn't have much to do with this topic. Maybe he wanted to believe it all, and this question was simply a hurdle for him. I attempted my amateur answer.

"Interesting that you asked. This observation of human behaviors was a question for me, and I believe it's probably a hurdle for many nonbelievers. Even though my experience didn't directly involve this topic, it did absolutely establish God's existence. Therefore, for my own peace of mind regarding why there is so much imperfection among the believers in God, I have done some amateur Bible research on the topic.

"Simply put, the physical world is a place where bad influence directed by Satan and his minions is allowed to exist and permeate all activity. Whether that was always the case, or it started with the famous disobedience of God by Adam and Eve as outlined in Genesis, it's a simple truth."

"Thanks for the Sunday school lesson, Glenn. I'm asking why today's Christians are so imperfect as humans."

"Well, Dr. Kyle, can we first agree that not all Christians behave exactly the same as each other? I have met some professing Christians who do seem nearly perfect regarding their actions and words matching their profession of salvation, whereas others seem to struggle with their behaviors."

"Sure, Glenn. I'm not saying they all behave the same. I'm asking your theory as to why they aren't perfect."

"I am unaware of any reference in the Bible to perfect humans, other than Jesus during his time in a human body, in which he seemed to always behave consistently with his own teachings. It seems to boil down to the fact that Jesus experienced physical body death as a sacrifice to purchase forgiveness of human bad behaviors (that is, sins), not to stop them from ever happening. Becoming a Christian means that one has obtained forgiveness of sins, but a Christian still faces every remaining day in his or her physical body, subject to the physical world inclinations, thoughts, and behaviors. And Satan has been allowed to be an influence within the minds of people residing in their physical bodies as part of the physical world."

"So you're saying that becoming a Christian gets you a ticket to a permanent paradise but does not require Christlike behavior?"

"Dr. Kyle, from what I've read and experienced, I would say it a little differently. It's true that when you make your deal with God and Jesus, you have obtained your ticket to the permanent paradise. However, until your physical body dies, you are still residing in a physical-world body, subject to the influence of Satan. Accepting Christ and His sacrifice with God's forgiveness adds a new perspective to one's thoughts and inclinations, which hopefully and usually does result in better behavior patterns. However, it does not make a person nonhuman. Christians usually need to ask forgiveness for various thoughts and behaviors for the remainder of their human lives. As long as they don't revert to denying God or Christ, they retain their ticket to heaven. However, what I just said about one's perspective changing when accepting Christ should be emphasized. Usually a person who becomes a Christian immediately experiences this change in perspective, and the new relationship with God and Jesus results in a new perspective with a change in inclinations, habits, and desires that alters one's behavior to be at least somewhat more Christlike."

"Why does this all-powerful God you met allow bad things to happen to good people?"

Interesting. Was the doctor becoming a believer based upon my experience, or was he just playing with me? "My experience gave me no direct insight into this common question. I am not a Bible scholar, and I believe there are some who could probably cite multiple enlightening scriptures on this topic."

"This is such an important question to so many questioners. You must have some thoughts about it."

"Okay, Dr. Kyle, here's the best my simple mind has for that question. Everyone knows that in our physical dimension, each and every physical body is destined to physically die, even if the person inhabiting that body did mostly good things while it was alive. Because every physical body is destined to die, then it is not logical to expect only good outcomes for every physical world experience for any physical body."

The professor expectantly looked at me like I wasn't finished. He outstared me, so I felt compelled to try something more.

"Everything was good in the physical world until the people listened to Satan and disobeyed God's rules for living in an all-good physical world. Since that act of disobedience, all humans face uncomfortable imperfections and various degrees of suffering while they are a part of the physical-world dimension."

"You mean to tell me that after this wild experience of yours, this is all you have for answers to this endearing theological question?"

I was stunned. My OBE confirmed God's existence. I didn't understand why he took the discussion in this direction. If he couldn't argue my experience away, was he simply attacking God's existence from another angle? I tried to go on.

"Well, I believe the biblical version is true. And my experience did give me perspective to more easily accept the biblical story of why there is bad or evil in our physical world. I kind of see it like God is to humans as parents are to their children. That is, our physical existence is only temporary, so no bad physical world experience is permanent, and we are to learn and grow from our physical world tribulations in preparation for the eternal life in paradise."

"Okay, Glenn. I've heard these arguments before, and I know there are many Bible verses along these lines. However, I'm looking for pure logic. For example, logic says that if only good things are happening to a person, then physical death is a bad thing because it stops all of the good things."

"But all physical death is not a bad thing. For some, physical death is a relief from bad things happening to them in the physical dimension."

"Don't disappoint me, Glenn. You are interrupting a perfectly good flow of logic. The second half is that if physical death is a relief, then it is an escape from the bad things that have happened to that person."

Now I understood. Wow. The professor already had a logical answer to his question, so clearly this endearing question was not his hurdle to believing in the existence of God. He must have been testing me in some way. I hoped I had not let him down and lost his interest in my experience.

"Okay," I responded. "I think I get it. Because physically dying has to be either a good thing or a bad thing for that person, it is logically impossible to have a complete physical life with only good things happening to you. Either bad things have happened, which makes dying a good thing, or only good things have happened, which makes physically dying a bad thing. And therefore all humans have to go through something bad before leaving the physical body."

"Exactly. And therefore it is a complete waste of energy and time to ponder the question of why bad things happen to good people. In fact, it is impossible for the bad things not to happen."

What in the world just happened? I had to ask. "Dr. Kyle, if you didn't have this question, why are you an atheist?"

"I have other reasons. I simply know that this question is a big hurdle to believing in God for many people, so I wanted to see what logic work you had done on it after your claimed encounter with God.

"I guess I fell a little short there."

"Now you have that little bit of logic to go with your encounter. And, I must say ..." He paused and leaned back in his chair. "The removal of that thought hurdle makes it much easier to allow your spiritual dimension experience to truly be accepted as related to the existence of God."

I'm glad you now have a second reason to believe my story. Remember, I've stated that I met God in that dimension. I would hope that is enough to believe me."

"Sorry, Glenn. I didn't mean to offend you. I meant using logic versus just accepting your word. I have another question for you. A lot of years passed between your encounter and today. It seems to me that if this is all true, you would've been sharing this encounter quite a bit over the years, and maybe even become ... I don't know, a Bible scholar or something like that. I'm wondering why not."

Wow. Although his question carried the potential of the setup for an attempted knockout blow, in a way this was the best reaction I'd seen from Dr. Kyle. At least his demeanor and tone seemed to be laced with more curiosity than skepticism.

"Well, Doctor," I responded, "as you recall, I have shared that at the time of the encounter, everyone else was skeptical, including the Christians with whom I did share it. There I was, with hard knowledge of God's existence and nature, yet there seemed to be no place for me among the world's believers. I spent many years in heavy discussions with God, but I saw myself as an outsider at whatever church I attended. I kept challenging God with questions about which scenario was real. Was he—"

"Whoa. I thought you confirmed God is real?"

"I did, and that's not what I meant that to sound like, if that's how those words came across. I simply wasn't done with my explanation, and I suppose I should've used the word *true* rather than *real*." At least I knew I had his rapt attention as long as he was jumping on my technical word usage.

"Sorry. Go ahead."

"Thanks. I was trying to say that even though I had firsthand knowledge of God being very real and very active, I was discouraged about those professing Christians shutting down my story. I did kind of try it with a couple of God skeptics, and as expected, they also discounted my story."

"Sounds like a setting for bringing on some real loneliness."

"Maybe, but I was never actually lonely, just frustrated. As I mentioned, I continued to carry on very heavy but private discussions with God, and I also carried on a very active social, work, and family life. I simply avoided churches where I felt out of place for reasons that no one around me realized. I knew God exists, and most of the churches I tried had people kind of hoping he exists but unwilling to hear me out. That made them, at that time for me, a frustrating group to be around. Then there were all of the work, business, social, and family people, among whom there were several God skeptics. I simply avoided discussing my experience, although I did assert that I believed in God when it came up."

"Okay, let's get back to your heavy discussions with God."

"Right. I was starting to say that I kept challenging Him to help me understand His nature. As I also mentioned, I clearly knew He existed, so to me, His nature was the only thing I needed to figure out, especially because the people I thought were His people had rejected my story."

"But you've been sharing with me all this stuff about the Bible and Jesus. What do you mean you were questioning the nature of God?"

"I'm trying to answer your question about all the years that transpired between my encounter and now. Please let me finish. It seems your habit of critical listening is overtaking your patience to hear this out." I hoped my firmness wasn't taking this discussion downhill, but he smiled and nodded. I continued.

"I actually spent energy trying to get God to confirm exactly what I ought to believe about His nature. I challenged whether He had just created everything and let it go without His further involvement, except in maybe a few instances when He feels like it. I also spent time asking Him why good things happen to bad people."

"Was there a reason you didn't simply accept that He was the God of the Judeo-Christian Bible?"

"I was just getting there. I did do some Bible reading, and I had spent some time reading about the yet unfulfilled prophecies. I had no reason to be unsure about the nature of God other than, first, His earthly people were rejecting my account, and second, I didn't see how these unfulfilled prophecies could ever come true."

"Are you talking about the end-time stuff?"

"Yes, but I call it the 'end of this era of earth history' stuff," I said with a smile. "In any event, I was struggling with these questions and staying quiet about my encounter for many years. I felt that if I couldn't support the story of these prophecies, then I had nowhere to take the story of my encounter if I brought it up."

"Are you justifying that position? If so, why are you now telling about your encounter?"

I felt like I could have finished my explanation by now if he hadn't kept interrupting me. But I didn't want to fall into the negativity of interacting about our conversation tactics. It's also true that I have a reputation for stringing out my stories, so I'll try to keep going as succinctly as possible.

"I'm definitely not justifying that position," I emphasized. "In fact, it led to me doing something I definitely do not recommend. I challenged God to answer me. The real relevant factor here is that I committed to jumping in with both feet into the Word of God and sharing my story if He would show me something to convince me that these prophecies can come true."

"Why are you not recommending that?"

Here we go again. He just can't let me go without interruption. I guessed the positive side of this was that he was showing genuine interest in, and at least seeming acceptance, of this whole supernatural experience.

"God is the heavyweight in this story. We are not on equal terms. He created the physical world and has supernatural control over it. Accepting that, and our subordinate role, is much more highly recommended than challenging the almighty God on our terms. Especially because all of our knowledge, abilities, and talents are given to us by God, which implies He and we are not on anything close to equal footing for us to lay down challenges to Him."

"Do you think you paid any kind of price for this 'not recommended' behavior?"

"I don't know, but I did go through some very difficult experiences. All humans go through something difficult for them in some way, so I don't know whether God was allowing that in my life because of my challenge or possibly my lack of sharing the encounter. However, I can tell you that just like God's qualities are deeper and more powerful than our best qualities, his supernatural patience is truly awe-inspiring.

"Now that I've explained my mindset that resulted in such a long delay in sharing my story, I'll share what changed all of that. Regarding those 'end of this era' prophecies, I'm sure you are aware that an antichrist character comes on the scene, the people follow him even though he is evil possessed, and his statements are lined with deceit."

Dr. Kyle nodded, so I kept going.

"Well, I believed that at least a majority of the population, even in tyrant-ruled countries, knows truth and goodness from evil. Therefore, I had real trouble accepting that this character could ever gain control, supported by the general population. Here's where the challenge came in, and I let it set between God and me. Again, His patience and timing are perfect, and mine are not.

"Talk about patience and timing. It was a couple decades after I spoke my challenge to God, which was long, long after the encounter, that I got my answer."

"Did you have another OBE that resolved your question?" Dr. Kyle inquired.

"No, but I am very fortunate that God did interact with my life to very specifically and directly answer my challenge." I paused, anticipating some sort of challenge from him. He smiled, and I didn't wait for his comment as I continued. "I happened to be watching a certain TV channel at a certain time when it happened. Suddenly, what I saw sent chills up my spine. I'm not going to tell the detailed specifics because I don't want to drag us into a discussion regarding world politics. I never contacted the network for a copy to confirm whether I saw exactly what they presented, or whether these few moments of presentation had been supernaturally altered for me. That doesn't really matter, because the bottom line is that I saw something that instantly and dramatically made it crystal clear how an antichrist character can come into control of large swaths of the population. The hair stood up on the back of my neck as the atmosphere around me and the feelings within me were suddenly altered. The exhilaration brought me to my feet. I was consumed with the absolute knowledge that God had just answered my challenge from a couple of decades earlier. I immediately went scrambling to find a book about the prophecies that I hadn't opened for many years."

"Glenn, this is an exhilarating story, but a lot of people periodically get inspirations."

"I realize that, because I have had my share of inspirations as well. Trust me, this was very different from the chills we may get from an inspiration, or having a light bulb click on in our minds. Every particle of the atmosphere around me changed with the presence of the Almighty. Besides that, you haven't heard the rest.

Although I did acknowledge to God that I understood His message and thanked Him for bothering to have anything to do with me, I simply walked around the next few days thrilled but searching for a specific direction. Then three days later, God delivered step two."

"Step two?"

I shrugged with a pleading facial expression and held out my hand palm up to say, "Let me finish, please." He nodded and gestured back to me.

"I woke up three days later and turned on the TV, and there it was. A famous Christian pastor and author talking about Bible prophecies. After first getting another case of the chills, I was especially pleased because this person was speaking intellectually and rationally about the prophecies, not emotionally or with limited logic, as I had heard in some churches decades earlier."

"Why can't this be a coincidence?"

"I understand your question, but once again, I'm not done yet. Also, I was there and know that I wasn't even searching through channels, and I had no history of ever previously listening to this speaker. He simply presented on the screen, talking about the prophecies when I turned on the TV.

"Then God delivered step three."

"Okay, you've got me going again." He smiled.

"Yes, even though I clearly understood these messages were being presented to me in answer to my long-standing questions and challenge, I was still looking for more specific direction. As it turned out, this speaker I saw on TV didn't live all that far from me. I had a habit of getting up early, conducting my business online for a while, and then going to the fitness center closest to my house around 9:00 a.m. While there, three days after the seeing the speaker on TV, I suddenly heard this voice behind me saying with humor, a chuckle, and seeming existing friendship with some of the people there, "What are you guys doing here this time of day? Don't you have work to do? I'm only here now because my schedule was interrupted this morning." I thought I recognized the voice, and sure enough, when I turned around, there was the famous TV speaker, pastor, and intellectual prophecy teacher standing there. Trust me, I had no doubt why he was there at that time when he never usually came at that time. It turned out that even though we had been working out at the same place for six years, we had never seen each other there until that day. I engaged him in conversation, and later I began attending his church. His rational, intellectual teaching from the Bible was what I needed to complete this picture and the answer God had delivered to my challenge."

"So you must have then told him about your encounter?"

"Not yet. I saved that breakout moment for the most logic-bound, confirmed atheist I could find—you."

"Wow, Glenn. I'm not sure whether that is some sort of compliment or something else. We've spent a lot of time discussing this. This has been very interesting. I will give it some more thought and get back to you."

=12=

RETURN VISIT

And Jesus said to him, "I am the way, the truth, and the life. No one comes to the Father except through Me."

—John 14:6 (NKJV)

I did get a call from the professor a while later, but I was traveling. When I got back, he was unavailable. I figured he had heard me out and moved on.

I moved quite a distance away later, and after a couple years, I was in the area again on a visit and thought I would swing by.

When I approached the professor's office, there was a large group of students outside. One of them spoke up. "Are you here to join our group today?"

I asked, "what group"?

"The Bible study group," he said. "The professor is leading a series called 'Logic and God.'"

"I must be at the wrong place," I responded.

"O ye of little faith," came the familiar voice from behind me. "I tried to reach you, but I couldn't find you."

I stood there at a loss for words, trying to comprehend what I was witnessing.

"Yeah," he continued. "I have concluded that we will actually have bodies in heaven, and although they may look like our physical bodies, they will have some different key characteristics. What's the matter, cat got your tongue?"

All I could say was, "Wow!"

He went on. "I figure that where you went in your Descartes experience was some sort of general dimension with pretty general access. After hearing your story, I was motivated to do some additional research, and my perspective changed. It now seems so obvious to me that our souls exist permanently and are destined for another dimension based upon what we choose to believe. The bottom line is that further reading has lead me to the conclusion that once our physical bodies die, we want our souls to be welcomed into God's home for us, which is a specific all-good dimension where we get new bodies that don't age or die. In order to be welcomed there, we have to believe the God-Jesus story in the Bible, and consciously join a very personal relationship between our soul and God. It is all very logical, and therefore I have accepted the truth of Jesus's sacrifice for my sins. Further, I have become motivated to assist others in logical analysis of it all."

I was in shock and dumbfounded. I attempted to gather myself and reached out to shake his hand.

With a big smile on his face, he grabbed it firmly and said "Thanks for sharing your story with me!"

CONCLUSION

As mentioned in the introduction, the out-of-this-world experience at the heart of the preceding pages is described in detail, precisely the way it happened, including the encounters with the most powerful of super-human beings. There are no embellishments, nor is any part of that fateful experience omitted.

The conversations with the professor serve to provide the medium for sharing the facts of that experience as well as its ramifications and implications for our human life on earth and spiritual well-being.

I was compelled to write about this experience by powers beyond myself. The main purpose is to share in detail, with no embellishment, my testimony of this out-of-body experience with the spiritual-world interactions. The absolute knowledge of God's existence is a very powerful thing. Hopefully, the presentation of the brief discussion of the implications will help make the most powerful truth more easily acceptable and guide readers to punch their ticket to permanent paradise if they have not already done so—especially because Jesus so clearly outlined how simple it is to alter one's future on such a permanent basis.

As for those who may have doubts about the inclination of God to overtly interact with us while we are in our human bodies, I can guaranty that He does. God can obviously do anything He decides to do with any person He chooses whenever He feels like it. Based upon other experiences following this out-of body journey, I have become witness to many overt interactions between God and humans.

Printed in the United States
By Bookmasters